CW00530004

I WISH S
WOULD EXPLAIN
HEBREWS
TO ME!

I WISH SOMEONE WOULD EXPLAIN HEBREWS TO ME!

Stuart Olyott

THE BANNER OF TRUTH TRUST

THE BANNER OF TRUTH TRUST
3 Murrayfield Road, Edinburgh EH12 6EL, UK
P.O. Box 621, Carlisle, PA 17013, USA

*

© Stuart Olyott 2010

*

ISBN-13: 978 1 84871 060 3

*

Typeset in 11/15 Adobe Caslon Pro at
the Banner of Truth Trust, Edinburgh

Printed in the U.S.A. by
Versa Press, Inc.,
East Peoria, IL

To Ho Eng Ghee and Linda

and to all others who both live
and preach the gospel in Malaysia

CONTENTS

Preface

*E*very Christian needs to understand Hebrews. If they do not, they will misunderstand the Old Testament and will also fail to fully appreciate what our Lord Jesus Christ has done, what he is doing now, and what he is going to do in the future. As a result, they will remain spiritually stunted.

Over the years, plenty of books have been written to explain Hebrews, but only a few of them have had ordinary Christians in mind. Some of them are so large and so complicated that they appear to be the last word. Experts enjoy books like these, but everybody else is left bewildered.

The book in your hands does not aim to be 'the last word' but perhaps, for some, it will be useful as 'the first word'. I have tried to explain Hebrews as clearly as the subject matter allows, always remembering the advice of Albert Einstein that 'things should be as simple as possible, but no simpler'. Not only so, but it seems to me that it is not enough to explain the text; we also need to know how its teaching must be worked out in practice. You will therefore find that this book contains many applications, some of which are very direct.

I do not know how many commentaries on Hebrews I have read. I began making notes on the epistle over forty years ago and it is no longer clear to me where most of my insights have come from. I do remember, however, that I have long been deeply indebted to W. H. Griffith Thomas,[1] Thomas Hewitt,[2] and Irving

L. Jensen[3] in steering my way through the book, and I am glad to be able to acknowledge this publicly. You will hear echoes of their work everywhere.

If this modest book causes some of Christ's people to focus on him in a new way, and to follow him with renewed courage, my prayers for it will have been more than answered.

STUART OLYOTT
Connah's Quay,
North Wales,
September 2009

BEFORE WE BEGIN

It is about the year A.D. 65. It is just thirty-five years or so since our Lord was crucified, since he rose from the dead and ascended into heaven, and since he sent the Holy Spirit to his church on the Day of Pentecost. There are still lots of believers alive who can remember all this. They cannot forget what they saw and experienced for themselves!

Even some of the original apostles are still alive. However, most Christians are now second-generation believers. They have come to believe through the preaching and witnessing of the original eye-witnesses, or of those already converted in this way.

In Jerusalem the temple still stands, although there are hints in this letter that its days are numbered and that it will soon be gone (see, for example, 12:27). In the meantime, the Jewish religion goes on as before. But not all Jews are following the old ways. Great numbers of them have become Christian believers, and it is to a group of such believers that this letter has been written.

The letter does not tell us precisely where the members of this group are to be found. They seem to belong to a single congregation, but where are they? Do the many mentions of the temple, and its rites and sacrifices, suggest that they are in Jerusalem? Or does 13:24 suggest that they are in Italy?

What?

Those questions we cannot answer. But we are in no doubt at all about what has prompted the letter that has now come to them. Its readers are not in a good state. Their new-found faith in Christ is in danger of petering out (3:12-14). They are not as keen as they used to be. In fact, some of them are not even bothering to come to church (10:25), while many who do come are not paying much attention to the preaching (2:1). Their level of interest is going down and down.

It seems that the whole group is open to discouragement. Their hands are hanging down (12:12). Instead of being keen and able to teach the faith to others, they are showing little interest in going forward in the Christian life. They have not even mastered the ABC of the gospel, let alone its more advanced truths (5:12). Things are so bad that they now actually need someone to come to their church and to teach them again the most basic things of all!

What a change has come over them! It is not that long ago that they stood firm in the fires of persecution and did not flinch (10:32-34). It is not like that now. They have begun to weaken. If they were still practising Jews, the Roman Empire would recognise them as members of a legally-recognised religion. But they are Christians, and it is Christians that Nero has recently been imprisoning, murdering and burning. Would it not be better to give up Christianity and to return to Judaism? Why be branded as a criminal when what you did before was legal? Why not take the easier road? And so it is that these believers are toying with the idea of giving everything up. At this point a letter arrives at their church. Praise God, it will help them all to put such a ruinous idea out of their heads.

Who?

Who is the letter from? What was clear to the original readers is not immediately clear to us, because the writer does not give his name. Paul is the most likely candidate. There are lots of similarities between his other letters and this one, both in style and content. Everything is centred on the person and work of Christ. In addition, the writer has a close and affectionate link with Timothy (13:23). What seems to clinch it, however, is the fact that the author's final sentence is, 'Grace be with you all' (13:24). Every one of Paul's letters ends with some sort of similar benediction. Closing prayers for grace are his unique signature tune (see *2 Thess.* 3:18).

The Christian church has had a long history, and the centuries bear witness that most scholars have accepted Paul as the author of Hebrews. The reason he throws some people off the scent by some changes in style, yet plays his signature tune without signing his name, is probably something to do with the awful persecution going on at the time. In the Second World War many Allied broadcasts went out to continental Europe using varying wavelengths, but particular tunes were used in the programmes so that discerning listeners could identify their source and pick up hidden messages encoded within them.

In such circumstances those who do not recognise the tune, or who cannot crack the code, are left guessing. Guesses about who may have written Hebrews include Apollos, Aquila, Barnabas, Luke, Silas, Philip the deacon and Clement of Rome. The list is actually much longer than this, but we do not need to pay any attention to it. The fact is that if Hebrews had not been written by an apostle, or by someone writing under the supervision or influence of an apostle, the early church would never have accepted it as Scripture. But it accepted it with very little hesitation. Early Christians hummed tunes which many others have never learned.

Why?

The purpose of the letter is obvious. The faith of the Hebrews is like a fire that has been dampened down. It is still smoking a little, but there is no flame. As you dig under the surface you at last find a few warm embers. If you leave them as they are, they will go out completely. So you put on a little hay and tinder and, once there is a crackle or other sign of life, you gently but firmly fan it all up. Before long there is a visible flame which, if given even more air and fuel, eventually becomes a blaze. The apostle writes his letter to rekindle the Hebrews' dampened fire. What a letter! It is worth reading by any believer whose spirit is fainting, whose enthusiasm is dying, and whose hearing has become dull.

The fuel that the apostle puts on the smouldering fire is his teaching. The opening verses introduce us to the central subjects that he will cover in his letter. He speaks of *revelation:* 'God . . . spoke' (1:1). He speaks of a *person:* 'God . . . has . . . spoken to us by his Son' (1:1-2). He speaks of a *work:* 'he . . . by himself purged our sins' (1:3). This, in summary, is what the Epistle to the Hebrews is about.

The way the apostle fans up the fire is by warning and exhortation. Five times he breaks off from his teaching to give solemn warnings: 'Take heed . . . do not miss the promised rest . . . beware of laziness and apostasy . . . beware of wilfully sinning . . . make sure that no one falls short of the grace of God' (2:1-4; 3:7-4:1; 6:4-8; 10:26-31; 12:12-17, 25-29). On countless occasions he exhorts his readers, saying 'let us' do this, or 'let us' do that (for example, 4:1, 11, 16; 6:1; 10:22-24; 12:1, 28; 13:13,15). This is an epistle that speaks directly to the conscience.

Structure

This balance of teaching and exhortation explains the structure of the letter. There are thirteen chapters in all. From the beginning up to 10:18 it is mostly teaching; from 10:19 to the end it is mostly exhortation. The epistle, then, is made up of two main sections.

In the first section, up to 10:18, the apostle is answering the key questions which the Hebrew believers are asking: 'Why shouldn't we go back to Judaism? What do we have as Christians which we did not have before?' The writer seems to be saying, 'Let me show you what we have.' He then tells them of the Lord Jesus Christ, the divine priest, the redeemer-priest, the apostle-priest, the perfect priest, the eternal priest. 'We have such a high priest' is his triumphant message (8:1).

10:19-25 summarises the rest of the book: 'Therefore, brethren, having . . . let us . . .' From 10:19 the apostle proceeds mainly to exhortation, all of which is based on the glorious truth, 'We have such a high priest.'

What To Look For

As we work through the book of Hebrews by means of this simple commentary, our study will be enriched if we note a number of its key features.

There are some key *words*. One which is particularly obvious is 'better'. The apostle will use this several times as he shows to us that Christ is superior to the prophets, to the angels, to Moses, to Joshua, and to Aaron. Other key words are 'perfect', 'eternal', 'partaker', 'heavenly', 'blood', 'faith', 'sacrifice', 'covenant', 'Son', 'high priest', 'ministry', and 'love'.

There are some key *topics*. These are the person of Christ (who he is), the work of Christ (what he has done, what he is doing, and what he is yet to do), the relationship of the old and new covenants, the sins of unbelief and disobedience, faith, testing and discipline, and how we are to measure spiritual growth.

There are some key *contrasts*. What are the differences between the following—the Son of God and the angels of God? God's servant, Moses, and God's Son, Jesus? Canaan's rest and God's rest? Aaron's priesthood and Christ's priesthood? Spiritual infancy and spiritual maturity? Apostasy and perseverance? Old Testament sacrifices and Christ's sacrifice? Faith and sight? Mount Sinai and Mount Zion? When we have finished the book, we should be clear about all of this.

Importance

Who can ever calculate the importance of the Epistle to the Hebrews for Christians today?

Do you have trouble understanding the Old Testament? Hebrews is the best commentary on the Old Testament that has ever been written. It interprets its history. It explains the fulfilment of its prophecies. It reveals the purpose that lies behind all its institutions of worship. It is especially valuable in helping us understand the Book of Leviticus by showing to us the significance of its complicated rituals—those ceremonies and sacrifices were types pointing forward to Christ, the great sacrifice for sin, the true priest, and the one mediator between God and man.

Are you confused about what the Lord Jesus Christ is doing now? Many believers are very hazy about this. Hebrews tells us about his intercession, explaining what it is and why it is necessary. Not only so; but just as Jehovah brought his people out of Egypt, through the wilderness, and into the promised land, in the same way the Lord Jesus Christ, who delivered us, is taking us safely through our life's journey. He is protecting us, supplying our needs and training us, and will eventually (but certainly) bring us into his heavenly glories!

Do you sometimes get tired of the Christian life? On this point you will find that Hebrews is very searching. It is possible, despite your claims, that you are not a true believer at all; you have the right words, but you do not actually have what the Bible promises. Or perhaps you are a true believer who has become a backslider. Or maybe you are someone who is tempted to turn away from simple faith in the Lord Jesus Christ, being inclined to think little of the glory of his person and work, and to compare other religions and ideas favourably with the gospel.

This great epistle is the answer to all these conditions. It shows us the folly of going back to our former life, because the unspeakably wonderful blessings that are found in Christ cannot be found anywhere else. In one way and another, again and again, it says to us, 'Consider him' (12:3). The antidote to every spiritual illness is a better sight of Christ. It is the medicine that cures all spiritual troubles. So it is that Hebrews concentrates on holding him up in all his glory and dignity, in all the beauty of his person and the wonder of his work. Stand back in awe and love! Look at him! Reflect on his deity, his humanity, his sacrificial work, his priestly office, and his kingly majesty. Look at him, as he is presented to us in this book. Get to know him better than before. Then you will never leave him.

How sad it is to see Christians looking over their shoulders at what they have left behind and longing to go back to it; to see them regretting that they once turned their back on the world; to see them disappointed that they have become followers of Christ! But we must be careful; none of us is immune to such lukewarmness. We must all take steps not to fall into apostasy. That is why every one of us needs to study the Letter to the Hebrews.

2

GOD HAS SPOKEN

PLEASE READ HEBREWS 1:1-4

H as your appetite been stirred up a little? Do you feel that you would now like to get better acquainted with the epistle that we have spoken about in the introduction? If so, we can begin right away.

How will such a wonderful and helpful letter open? The apostle launches straight into his subject. He begins by assuring us of four things and, in doing so, prepares our minds for all that is to follow. Let us see what they are.[1]

1. The fact of a divine revelation: God has spoken (1:1-2)

There is a God. This is not a point that anyone needs to argue about. Your own conscience knows that it is true.

We do not have to guess what God is like. He has spoken! The truth is not that any man or woman has discovered him, but that he has revealed himself. He has made himself known.

This being so, it is obvious what our greatest duty is. It is not to wonder, to speculate, to dispute, to philosophise or to guess, but to listen to what God has revealed about himself, and to obey. The question we mortals should be asking is not, 'How can these things be?' but rather, 'What exactly has God said?'

2. The reality of the Old Testament as a divine revelation (1:1)

The Old Testament is a real divine revelation; 'God . . . spoke in time past'. However, we must note that he did not speak on only one occasion. He did not say everything he had to say in one fell swoop. He spoke 'at various times'. The Old Testament is a progressive revelation. God revealed something; then he was silent. Later on he spoken again; then he was silent. This is the way it went on through the centuries, as he revealed more, then more, then more.

God did not always reveal himself in the same way. Sometimes he spoke with an audible voice. Once he wrote something with his own finger. Sometimes he used visions. More usually, his Spirit came upon a man in such a way that that man expressed his thoughts in words which were exactly those that God had intended. One revelation followed upon another, but each one was incomplete. For example, Abraham heard God speak; this was a privilege experienced years later by Moses, and David, and others. Each one knew that they had not received God's final word, because the promised Messiah had not yet come. But they did not know when God would speak again, or precisely when his final revelation would be given.

Nobody must despise or devalue the Old Testament. But nor must anyone overvalue it. It is a genuine divine revelation, but the way that revelation came was sporadic, fragmentary, varied, progressive—and incomplete!

As he opens his letter, it is important for the apostle to mention all this. His readers are thinking about giving up their Christianity and going back to Judaism. They need to know, right from the beginning, that if they do this, they will be going back to an incomplete revelation. It is true that God has spoken in the Old Testament. But that Old Testament does not contain all that he has to say. It is only part of the picture.

3. The superiority of Christ as a divine revelation (1:2a)

'In these last days' God has spoken again. The apostle, of course, is writing in Greek, and we can also translate his words like this: 'at the end of these days'. In other words, God has spoken again, but this time his revelation is his last one. Now that this last revelation has been given, he has nothing more to say.

This revelation is not fragmentary, but complete. It is not temporary, but permanent. It is not preparatory, but final. It has not come through various means, but is embodied in the person who is supreme.

God's revelation in the Lord Jesus Christ is superior in character, because it is complete. It is superior in time, because no revelation will follow it. It is superior in destination, because it is to us. It is superior in agent because, unlike the Old Testament, which came through feeble human prophets, it has come through God's Son.

Notice that there is continuity between the Old and New Testaments, but there is also a contrast. Jesus is not the instrument of God; he is God himself. The final word that God has spoken to the world is through his Son. The word 'Son', found here, is central to the whole of the Epistle to the Hebrews. It occurs seven times, and always at crucial points in the apostle's argument.

4. The proofs of Christ's superiority (1:2-4)

The apostle could have gone straight in to tell us what God has said through his Son. This is what we would have expected. Instead he bursts into a description of the Son's glories. He does this to show us that the revelation of God through his Son really is superior to anything experienced or known before.

He tells us seven things about him. Seven is an important number in the Bible. It is the number of perfection. So the apostle tells us seven things about the Son as a further way of underlining in our minds that Christ is perfect, both in himself and as a revelation of the Godhead. We see him as:

(i.) *Christ the heir* (verse 2)

Imagine a very rich person who has only one son. What happens to his riches when he dies? They go to his son, as also do all his titles and privileges. Everything is now in the son's hands and all eyes are upon him. Of course, God the Father cannot die. But the apostle uses this picture to help us grasp that everything that belongs by right to God, belongs to Christ. In particular, Christ is the crown, the climax and the consummation of history. The whole future belongs to him. The time is coming when every eye will be fixed on him and will see who he really is.

(ii.) *Christ the creator* (verse 2)

Christ is the end of everything, but he is also the beginning! The Greek of verse 2 tell us that he is the one 'through whom [God] made the ages'. In other words, not only are the beginning and the end in Christ's hands, but so also is everything in between. *This* is the one through whom God has spoken in these last days!

(iii.) *Christ the revealer* (verse 3)

We are now told who Christ is eternally; what he is in himself, before anything else existed. He is 'the brightness of [God's] glory and the express image of his person'. He is the effulgence, the irradiated brightness of God. He is the exact representation of his being. In its essence, Godhood, God-ness, is invisible. It can only be known by someone whom the Father is eternally begetting. Nobody can see, has ever seen, or will ever see, the Father. You see him by looking at the glorious second person of the Trinity who is God in his own right, and yet is eternally streaming from the Father. Whenever anyone has seen anything of God or experienced anything of God, it is Jesus Christ that they have seen and experienced.

(iv.) *Christ the sustainer* (verse 3)

We are now told what is Christ's relationship with the universe. What stops it from disintegrating or going out of existence? What power holds all its atoms and molecules together? Moment after moment, year after year, century after century, it continues to exist. What is the explanation? The universe's continued existence is not something that just 'happens'. Christ's word brought it into existence; a word from him will end it all; and it is that same word of his that holds it all together. Paul puts it like this in Colossians 1:17: 'in him all things consist'.

(v.) *Christ the redeemer* (verse 3)

This glorious person whom the apostle is describing is the redeemer of believers!

> He came down to earth from heaven
>   who is God and Lord of all,
> and His shelter was a stable,
>   and His cradle was a stall.
> With the poor, and mean, and lowly
>   lived on earth our Saviour holy.[2]

But he did more than that. All alone, he went to the cross, bled and died there, and by this act 'purged our sins'. He put away the sin of every believer of every age. He cleansed their record. He destroyed every obstacle that debarred them from fellowship with God by making them pure in his eyes. My sins have been dealt with by a person—the person whom these verses describe in all his magnificence—the one through whom God has spoken in these last days!

(vi.) *Christ the ruler* (verse 3)

He went to the cross, but where is Christ now? He is not dead, but risen; not only risen, but ascended; not simply ascended, but glorified. The eternal Son of God, who became a man, sits as the God-Man in the place of his former glory, 'the right hand of the Majesty on high.' He is sitting down, because he has completed the work that he came to do. No Old Testament priest ever sat down during his duty, because his work was never finished. How different Christ is! His once-for-all, never-to-be-repeated sacrifice is over. It is finished.

(vii.) *Christ the supreme* (verse 4)

No angel, even the most exalted one of all, would dare to sit down in God's presence, let alone at his right hand. But Christ is higher than the highest angel. Unlike them, he is not a servant; he is the eternal Son. The place where he sits is the highest in the universe, and it is his by right. It is his inheritance. Such is our Lord Jesus Christ, who is prophet (through whom God speaks; verse 2), priest (by whom sinners come to God; verse 3) and king (reigning as God; verses 3-4).

If you have never come to Christ, it is to *this* Christ that you have never come. If you heart is cold towards Christ, it is towards *this* Christ that you are cold. And if you are thinking of deserting Christ, it is *this* Christ that you are considering deserting!

To turn away from Christ is always to turn away from the greatest to something less—much, much less. It is to turn from the most glorious of all to the shoddy. It is to turn your back on the radiance of God's glory in order to walk into outer darkness.

> His name is Wonderful, His name is Wonderful,
> His name is Wonderful, Jesus my Lord.
> He is the Mighty King, Master of everything,
> His name is Wonderful, Jesus my Lord.
> He's the Great Shepherd, the Rock of all Ages,
> Almighty God is He;
> Bow down before Him, love and adore Him,
> His name is Wonderful, Jesus my Lord.[3]

3

TEACHING AND WARNING

PLEASE READ HEBREWS 1:5-2:4

The apostle, then, is writing to men and women who are seriously thinking of giving up the Christian life and going back to what they were before. He approaches their problem by parading before them the glories of Christ. If you walk away from him, you are turning your back on the radiance of God's glory and walking into outer darkness.

The passage now before us is composed of two parts. 1:5-14 is teaching; 2:1-4 is warning.

1. Teaching (verses 5-14)

The purpose of this paragraph is to expand the phrase 'better than the angels' which the apostle has just used in verse 4. As Jews, the first readers of this letter thought a lot of angels. One of the reasons that they had such reverence for the laws God gave at the time of Moses was that they had come to them by means of angel intermediaries. Stephen mentions this fact in Acts 7:53, as does Paul in Galatians 3:19. How wonderful! It is important, then, that the apostle should show them that Christ, the centre of the gospel, is greater than these angels. If he does not, how will he be able to persuade them to remain loyal to Christ rather than return to Judaism?

The argument the apostle uses would have had great power with his Jewish readers. He quotes seven verses from their Scriptures, one of which is from 2 Samuel, while the rest are from the Book of Psalms. In doing so, he succeeds in making four points, all of which combine to make his central point—Jesus is better than the angels; he is far superior to them.

(i.) *Angels are merely angels: Christ is the Son* (verses 4-5)

Christ is greater than the angels because he has a better name than they do (verse 4). Never once did God say to an angel 'You are my Son.' Only to Christ, and of Christ, did he say this. The beginning of verse 5, which quotes Psalm 2:7, refers to his eternal generation. This is a mystery which we can describe in words, but which we can never truly understand. By 'eternal generation' we mean that everything Christ is, he owes to the Father, even though he is God in his own right. He is eternally begotten of the Father. This is happening now, has always been happening, and will never cease to happen. No angel enjoys such a relationship with God the Father.

The second half of verse 5, which quotes from 2 Samuel 7:14, continues to refer to the relationship which exists between the first and second persons of the Trinity. In their original context, these words refer to Solomon; but every Jew recognised Solomon as a type and prefiguration of the Messiah to come, and so would not have been surprised at how the words are used here. Angels, being merely messengers (the word 'angel' also means 'messenger'), are never addressed with such dignity. They are sent by God, but they are not God. It is obvious, therefore, that to go from a religion centred around the Son in order to re-enter a religion rejoicing in angels would be a backward and retrograde step.

(ii.) *Angels are merely worshippers: Christ is the one who is worshipped* (verse 6)

The apostle has spoken of Christ's eternal being; he now mentions his coming into the world. He is described as 'the firstborn'. This important word, often used in the Old Testament, does not necessarily refer to the first child of the family to be born. Sometimes 'the firstborn' was not 'the first-to-be-born'! The word describes, rather, the senior member of the family, the one who will take over as head when the father has died. God the Father cannot die. Jesus Christ is, nonetheless, his 'appointed heir', as we have already been told in verse 2. In the context, the term refers to Christ's eternal deity as Son of God.

In Psalm 97:7 quoted here, which every Jew accepted as a reference to the coming Messiah, all the angels of God are commanded to worship him. When it comes to their glory, angels may well be superior to men; but the fact that Christ has become a man does not make them superior to him. Considering who he is, they are obviously infinitely below him in nature and in power. Their calling is to worship him and to serve him. In Isaiah chapter 6, the prophet saw them doing just that (because it was Christ that Isaiah saw there, as John 12:41 makes clear). In the same way, they publicly announced his birth (*Luke* 2:8-20), ministered to him in the desert (*Matt.* 4:11), strengthened him in Gethsemane (*Luke* 22:43) and, if requested by him, would gladly have delivered him from his cross (*Matt.* 26:53). Christ is so much greater than the angels.

(iii.) *Angels are merely creatures: Christ is the creator* (verses 7-12)

Verse 7, which quotes Psalm 104:4, contains two concepts, both of which display that angels are inferior and subordinate beings. They are creatures; God 'makes' them into something. They are servants, in the way that wind and fire are his servants. How they contrast with Christ, who, as the eternal Son of God, is neither of these things!

This Christ is addressed as God and sovereign. Verses 8-9 quote Psalm 45:6-7, which is a Messianic psalm where 'great David's greater Son'[1] is seen as the king who rides prosperously and rides eternally. The qualities of his reign are justice, righteousness and hatred of wickedness. To his throne, Christ has been anointed ('Christ' means 'anointed') rather than appointed. Could there be any clearer reference to the deity of Christ than this? How, then, can he ever be compared with the angels?

But how can Christ, who is addressed as God (verse 8), have someone as his God (verse 9)? To answer this, we must have the whole of the Bible in our minds. It teaches us that although there is but one God, there are three who are God (although there are not three gods!) The Father is God, the Son is God, the Holy Spirit is God; and each of these is God in the same sense. Of these, the Father is first, the Son is second, and the Holy Spirit is third, and yet there is neither senior nor junior. Not only so, but the Son, without ceasing to be God, became a man. As the second person of the Trinity, he has God the Father as his God from all eternity; as a man, he also has God as his God. All this is mind-baffling for us poor creatures. The right thing for us to do is not to speculate, but to accept the truth and to adore.

Next, in verses 10 to 12, the apostle quotes Psalm 102:25-27. Here Christ is addressed by the divine name of 'LORD' and spoken of as the creator, the one who remains unchangeable in the midst of things that change. These verses span the whole of history, showing that Christ existed before creation (and is therefore from eternity), carried out creation, will outlast creation, and will continue to exist for ever. Could any angel ever be spoken about like this?

(iv.) *Angels are merely servants: Christ is king* (verses 13-14)

The Old Testament passage now in the apostle's mind is the opening verse of Psalm 110, another Messianic psalm. No angel has ever been told to sit at God's right hand, but that is precisely where Christ sits as he waits for his final triumph over his enemies. Just as Joshua called his generals to put their feet on the necks of his defeated enemies (*Josh.* 10:24), so Christ will be seen to have eternally vanquished every person and force that has ever defied him.

Nothing remotely like that has ever been said about any angel, and never will be. After all, what are angels? They are not persons in the Godhead. They are created spirits who have been sent out by God, not only to serve him, but also to serve Christians. How revealing and how comforting this is! At the moment we seem so low, and angels appear so mighty. But it is we who will 'inherit salvation', and not they. Although we are already saved, the final consummation of our salvation (the resurrection body, public acquittal at the final judgement, the heavenly glories, *etc.*) still awaits us. Angels are already as high as they can be; we have yet to be finally glorified. At that point 'we shall judge angels' (*1 Cor.* 6:3). But we shall never even begin to compare in glory with our Lord Jesus Christ, so how much will less will the angels do so! So why should anyone be tempted to leave him and to return to a religion centred around a set of rules given through angelic intermediaries?

As we look back at the seven Old Testament quotations selected by the apostle, it is interesting to notice their progression. They deal with Christ's eternal relationship with the Father, his coming into the world, his anointing by God, and his reign. We see him beginning and ending the world, seated, and reigning for ever over his enemies. Seven spells perfection. We have read a royal survey.

What are angels in comparison with him?

But the apostle does not leave things there. Having given this marvellous teaching, he proceeds to give his readers a serious warning.

2. Warning (2:1-4)

(i.) The danger they faced (verse 1)

God has spoken, in a final manner, by this Son. This being so, you would think that everyone aware of it would be craving to hear what God has said by him. You would think that they would be giving all their attention and faculties to hear and understand what God has so perfectly and finally said.

Not at all! The Hebrews' attention is elsewhere. God has spoken his final word to the world, but they are less interested in it than they should be. At the very moment that they should be giving the more earnest heed to it, they are drifting away.

The picture is that of a boat caught in a fast current, being swept out to sea and lost. In such circumstances the most fragile boat is safe, as long as it is fixed to the shore. The choice is between being fixed to the shore or perishing. This being so, you would think that the Hebrews would always be checking their moorings, always tying the knot tighter and always strengthening the ropes. Instead, these believers have got the idea that they will be safe on the other side of the river. Instead of checking the ropes, they are cutting them one by one. Now only one is left—and the knot on that one is beginning to slip! They must do something! Their only safety is in the Lord Jesus Christ. If they do not remain attached to him, they will slip away into eternal doom.

(ii.) *The warning he gave* (verses 2-4)

We can paraphrase what the apostle says next like this:

2:2: 'Yes, indeed, the Old Testament law was given by the mediation of angels who, as we have seen, are inferior creatures. That law carried penalties, and these were faithfully and strictly carried out.'

2:3: 'If those who did not keep that law were punished, how much more will those be punished who depart from the gospel! The gospel message was not given by angels, but by the Lord himself. Its truth was confirmed to us by those who heard him personally—by first-hand witnesses. The gospel is a great message, with a greater Giver, and greater confirmation; it is obvious that turning from it certainly means a greater punishment. Is there any way at all that we will escape from that?'

2:4: 'Not only so, but God was actively at work in the lives and activities of those early eye-witnesses. He authenticated their ministry by signs, miracles, powerful and extraordinary wonders, and other gifts of the Holy Spirit which he gave as he willed, so that no one could possibly doubt that what they heard was a divine message.

'If you could not ignore the lesser message and get away with it, how shall we escape if we neglect this great and glorious message of salvation? To fail to pay increasing attention to it is to call down God's judgement!'

It is the very greatness of the gospel that makes apostasy a peril. To walk out on any other system of belief is simply to walk out on a human idea. But the gospel is not like that. It is not one idea among many. God has spoken! His final word to mankind is embodied in his Son. Look who the Son is. There is no one greater.

To walk out on the gospel is to walk out on the greatest person in the universe—your Creator, your Judge, the one who will put his foot on all his enemies, and the only one who is whom there is salvation, because, all by himself, he made purification for our sins.

At this point in the epistle, every one of us needs to pause and consider what our relationship with Christ is like. Am I attached to him at all? If so, is my attachment to him stronger or weaker than it has been in the past?

We shall find out from this epistle that there are only two sorts of knots tying the mooring rope to the shore: there are those that are tighter than they used to be, and there are those which are looser and beginning to slip. It is possible to be a professing Christian right now, and yet to be lost. But how is it that some apparent believers drift away and end up as apostates? The answer lies in one word: neglect.

4

THE MAN CHRIST JESUS IS GREATER THAN THE ANGELS

PLEASE READ HEBREWS 2:5-18

In our study of the Epistle to the Hebrews we come now to 2:5-18. What a tremendous passage it is! It shows us that the Lord Jesus Christ became the Son of Man that we might become sons of God. He came to earth that we might go to heaven. He bore our sins that we might partake of his righteousness. He took *our* nature that we might have *his*. He became man in order to restore to us all that we lost in Adam's fall.

In his argument, the apostle has just shown his readers that Christ is God himself, and therefore greater than the angels. This being so, why would they ever consider going back to a religion that revelled in the fact that its law was given by angelic mediation?

However, knowing the Jewish mind-set as he does, he is aware that an objection would certainly have sprung to their minds: 'Very well, Jesus is greater than the angels. But, by becoming a man, he became *lower* than the angels; and then, in that condition, he was further humiliated by suffering. That being so, how can you go on arguing for his greatness?'

It is with this unspoken objection in mind that the apostle now sets out to show that Christ is not only greater than the angels as the Son of God, but also as the Son of Man. Jesus the *man* is greater than the angels! If you walk out on him, you cannot console yourself by saying that you have turned your back on one who is great as far as his divine nature is concerned, but not great as far as his human nature is concerned. The old Welsh hymn got it right:

> Great my Jesus in His Person,
> Great as God *and man* is He . . .[1]

It is that point that the author insists on throughout this section. He does it in two stages. In verses 5-13 he shows us that Christ's superiority is not cancelled by his *coming* among us as a man. In verses 14-18 he shows us that his superiority is not cancelled by his *suffering* for us as a man.

1. Christ's superiority is not cancelled by his coming among us as a man (verses 5-13)

The easiest way to grasp the author's argument is to attempt to paraphrase it:

2:5: 'I have told you earlier (1:14) that angels have been appointed to serve Christians, not to rule them. The same thing is true of "the world to come". Angels will never rule. They may appear to be superior to us at the moment, but this does not alter the fact that they are servants.'

2:6-7: 'It is God's purpose that man should rule, not angels. This is clear from the Old Testament. Let me refer you to Psalm 8:4-6. When you look up at the stars and consider the vastness of the universe, man appears to be quite insignificant. But he is not. God is mindful of him, and cares for him. He is, for a little while, lower in majesty than the angels. And yet God has given him a position, and put upon him a dignity, that he has not granted to any other creature. He is the very peak of God's creation, being made in his image. All other creatures are lower in order than he is—and that includes the angels!'

2:8: 'God has decreed that nothing is to be left outside man's sovereignty except God himself, and this decree has never been rescinded or withdrawn. The fact is, however, that we do not yet see man in that position. For example, death terrifies him, sin enslaves him, and the devil oppresses him.

2:9: 'But although we do not yet see man *as man* in the position that God intended for him, we *do* see a representative Man in that position. Let me underline his humanness by using his human name of Jesus. We see him. He has been in our valley of humiliation. He has identified himself with us. He has spent time lower than the angels. He has been through suffering and death.

'It was God's grace—his undeserved generosity—that sent Jesus among us. And he tasted death. By this I mean that he did not simply die, but that he tasted all the humiliation and bitterness of death. He knows what death is, because he has been through it. And he did this for every one.'

When the apostle says that Jesus died for 'every one', he cannot possibly mean that he died for every individual on earth. This would contradict the plain teaching of Scripture elsewhere, and would mean that every person's sins had been atoned for, resulting in the salvation of every single human being. We need to remember that the author is writing to Jews. He is stressing that Christ died for Gentiles, as well as for them.

No wiser words on Hebrews 2:9 have been written than those penned by Professor John Murray:

Of whom is the writer speaking in the context? He is speaking of the many sons to be brought to glory (ver. 10), of the sanctified who with the sanctifier are all of one (ver. 11), of those who are called the brethren of Christ (ver. 12), and of the children which God had given to him (ver. 13). It is this that supplies us with the scope and reference of the 'every one' for whom Christ tasted death. Christ did taste death for every son to be brought to glory and for all the children whom God had given to him. But there is not the slightest warrant in this text to extend the reference of the vicarious death of Christ beyond those who are most expressly referred to in the context. This text shows how plausible off-hand quotation may be and yet how baseless is such an appeal in support of a doctrine of universal atonement.'[2]

These comments are important, but it is even more important not to get carried away on this point. If we do, we will miss the heart of what the apostle is saying. He is not debating the extent of the atonement; he is asking where the humiliated Jesus is *now*, in order to stress that Christ *as man* is greater than the angels.

That Man, that real man, is 'crowned with glory and honour'. Let us stop reading for a moment. Let us pause to reflect on what we are being told. At this moment there is a man, a glorified man, in heaven; and he is receiving divine honours! Look at him! Worship him! As we do so, we find that certain thoughts become unthinkable—such as the idea that *as a man* he is inferior to the angels.

2:10: 'Not only so, but the work that Jesus accomplished on the cross was an act worthy of God. It is for God that all things exist, and by whom they exist. He is behind every single event that happens. His eternal purpose is that many members of the human race should become his sons, and that he should bring them safely to glory. He has chosen to bring this about by means of a file-leader—that is, by someone who walks the path in front of others and shows them the way. The file-leader is Jesus.

'It was entirely fitting that God should make the one who leads his people to salvation perfect, and that he should do this through sufferings. This does not mean that Jesus was *not* perfect, and that he had to be made so by his cross. How could such an idea be true, seeing that the Saviour is *God?* It means, rather, that Christ would have been completely ineffective as a Saviour without his sufferings. He had to go that way. There is no other way that he could have saved the "many sons" and brought them to glory.

2:11: 'There is union between Christ and those he saves. He is the one who sets them apart to be saved; they are the ones who are thus set apart. He is the older brother beating a path through the jungle; they are the ones who benefit from his work and who follow. Because of the way in which he is so intimately linked to those he saves, he is not ashamed to call them "brothers".

2:12-13: 'Let me prove this to you from three Old Testament quotations. Everyone admits that Psalm 22:22 is a Messianic psalm, and it is clear there that the Messiah looks upon all of God's people as his brothers. Isaiah 8:17 sees the coming Christ (Messiah) putting his trust in God, thus proving both his humanity and his identification with his brothers. The following verse, Isaiah 8:18 originally referred to Isaiah and his children, but do you not agree that it is a most suitable quotation to describe what our Lord Jesus Christ says of his people in heaven?'

Thus the apostle shows that there is no way that anyone can argue that the Lord Jesus Christ is inferior to the angels on the grounds that he came among us as a man:

• For man *as man* is not inferior to the angels.

• Christ, as a man, has been exalted, and is today receiving divine honours.

• He could not have saved anyone without becoming a man, but in doing so he fulfilled God's express purpose.

• By becoming a man he perfectly identifies himself with those he came to save, and presents them in heaven as his brothers and God's children.

• The conclusion implied, but not stated, is this: if you are thinking of walking out on Christ, it is *this* Christ that you will walk out on!

2. Christ's Superiority Is Not Cancelled by His Suffering for Us as a Man (2:14-18)

In this brief commentary we will often paraphrase the apostle's argument, believing that this is frequently the best way to grasp his train of thought. We have done it already, and now we will do it again.

2:14-15: 'Those for whom Christ died are human; they are flesh and blood. In order to save them, the divine Christ also became human. Not only so, but he died, and by that death he rendered the devil's power ineffective.

'Think about death for a moment. It is something that came upon the human race as a result of its listening to the devil in Eden. It is a direct result of the devil's activity. It has imposed upon every man and woman a bondage which we cannot break. We go through life terrified of it. How the devil must have laughed!

'But Christ has changed all that. He died a human death; on behalf of his people, he tasted its bitterness and damnation. He took it upon himself. And now, although human death remains, its sting and horror no longer remain. Christ has delivered us from the tyranny which the devil imposed upon us!

'This tyranny, notice, was not broken by an angel, but by the sufferings of Christ. What a phenomenal victory! How then can it be argued that by becoming a man, and particularly by suffering, that Christ is to be regarded as inferior to the angels?

2:16: 'To win this victory Jesus did not become an angel, but a descendant of Abraham—a Jew! That is how the work was done. And the point of it all was not that he might help angels, but humans.

2:17: 'This is why he had to be made like his brothers in every way. If he had not been made so, he could never have been the Saviour they needed. We need someone to bring us into favour with God— a High Priest. He must be compassionate, understanding our need.

He must be faithful, doing all that was required from God's side. He must make propitiation for our sins, turning away God's wrath and diverting it upon himself. Jesus became all that by becoming a man. He is exactly the Saviour we need.

2:18: 'It is precisely because he has spent time in our arena of suffering and temptation, and has himself experienced the pain of the most intense temptation, that he is able to help and rescue those who are in that arena today. It is precisely because he became a man that he is the Saviour that he is. As a result he is not to be looked down on (as you Hebrews are inclined to do), but to be honoured and fled to.

'Christ's superiority is not cancelled by his suffering for us as a man. No, no! In fact, it is by this suffering that his superiority is displayed. What no angel could ever do, he has done—by becoming a man and suffering.'

Once more, then, the superiority of Christ has been established in the minds of those who first read this epistle and, hopefully, in our minds too. We have studied a difficult passage, but its lessons are clear:

• God himself is engaged in bringing many sons to glory. He does this by means of a file-leader—a person who beats a path for others who, following, find that it leads them to heaven.

• Christ is our file-leader, but he is also our brother. He is setting us apart, and we are being set apart, for a marvellous future. So great is his love for us that, despite what we are, he is not ashamed of us.

• Our older brother has faced all our foes and has won deliverance for us. Death remains, but its sting has been drawn and its power has gone. We need not fear what men and women call 'death'; it is but the threshold of glory.

• Christ has taken hold of us with a grasp and a grip from which he will never release us. Every temptation we face is one that Christ has been through already. Every dark path we tread, he has already walked. There is nothing we face that he has not himself faced. There is no occasion when we cannot call on him for help and find it.

• Best of all, he has dealt fully with our sins, so that God's anger is for ever turned away from us. Our cause is represented in heaven by someone who understand us totally, and who is pleasing to God.

In comparison with who Jesus is, every angel pales into insignificance. There is no one greater than Christ, no one more glorious, and no one more honoured. To cling to him is to be perfectly safe at every moment in this life, and to be eternally saved in the next. To forsake him is to walk out on the all-glorious God-Man, and to reject the only one who can do helpless sinners good. It is to be without a guide in this life, to be without comfort at the moment of death, and to be without hope in eternity.

If we have Christ, we have everything; if we forsake him, we have nothing—*that* is the message of the Epistle to the Hebrews!

5

THE PERIL OF APOSTASY

PLEASE READ HEBREWS 3:1-4:1

The Hebrews are seriously considering giving up their commitment to the gospel of Christ in order to return to their
former Judaism. The apostle is writing to them to persuade them
to see things differently. His first two chapters have made it clear
where such a course of action will lead them, but now, even more
bluntly, he spells out to them the peril of apostasy.

The author has a number of different weapons in his armoury.
In the first verse he uses exhortation. From there, in verses 2-6, he
turns to teaching. Then, from verse 7 until 4:1, he gives himself
to warning. We shall follow his argument closely before drawing
from it a number of applications for ourselves.

1. Exposition

(i.) *Exhortation* (3:1)

3:1: 'In the light of what I have said, consider Christ Jesus. Fix your
thoughts on him—ponder, study, meditate. You are "holy", that is,
set apart. You have been set apart from others and set apart for
God. You are "brothers", members of a divine family of which Jesus
Christ is the older brother. This is because you have received a "calling" that others have not received; Christ has not called them by
his Spirit and they have not been transformed by the powerful
call of the gospel. How different you are! The origin of your call is

"heavenly". God himself has spoken into your souls, convinced you of your sin, brought you to understand the truth of the gospel, and moved you to embrace Jesus Christ by faith.

'Judaism looks back to Moses and Aaron. Moses is Judaism's apostle, because "apostle" means "someone sent", and he was the one whom God sent to be his law-giver. Aaron was the first high priest, the appointed mediator between God and the Israelites, and all Jewish priests are descended from him.

'In the gospel message, both these offices of apostle and high priest are united in one person, Christ (the appointed Messiah) Jesus (his human name). Consider him; I have already shown you in what ways he is greater and superior. Do not turn your back on him, as you are being tempted to do. Do not walk out on him. Do not finish with him. Spend time thinking about him.'

> Turn your eyes upon Jesus,
> Look full in His wonderful face;
> And the things of earth will grow strangely dim
> In the light of His glory and grace.[1]

(ii.) *Teaching* (3:2-6)

As we have explained, the mention of 'the apostle and high priest of our confession' would immediately make the first readers think of Moses and Aaron. Is the Lord Jesus Christ *really* greater than these two? The apostle will show that he is. All that he will say later on about our Lord's high priestly ministry will clearly reveal that he is greater than Aaron. But he does not wait to show that Christ is greater than Moses. This is the point of this paragraph of teaching.

3:2: The great thing about Moses was his faithfulness. He was trustworthy; he did what God entrusted him to do. If he had failed,

Pharaoh would never have heard God's word and Israel would have compromised by yielding to Pharaoh's demands. In addition, Israel would have drawn back at the Red Sea, would have returned to Egypt from the wilderness, and would never have reached the borders of Canaan and entered in.

But Moses *was* faithful! He was faithful 'in all his house'; that is, the Israelites were the people and family of God, and Moses was entirely trustworthy in the work that he did among them.

In the same way, Christ was faithful in all the work that God had sent *him* to do. If he had yielded to any temptations at all; if he had refused to suffer and to die; if he had left the Father's will undone, then no sinner anywhere would have been saved. But the Lord Jesus Christ was faithful, and so was Moses—and, notice, that is the order in which the apostle puts it.

3:3: But Christ is entitled to far more honour and respect than Moses, just as the architect is entitled to more respect than the house he builds.

3:4: This is because Jesus Christ is God, and it is God that has built all things, the house of Israel included.

3:5: Moses was faithful as a servant in that household, as we have seen. But Christ is not the servant of God, but his eternal Son, as we have also seen.

3:6: In any household the son and heir has a completely different status from the servants, and it follows that Christ is worthy of infinitely more honour than Moses.

And of course, the household being spoken about is not the ancient Israel of history, but the true Israel of which the nation was a picture. It is the company of people whose confidence and faith in Christ never fails; it is the men, women and children who never cease to rejoice in the hope on which they have set their hearts.

Verse 6 would have surprised many of the original readers, just as it surprises very many readers today. The fact is that we are not members of God's family and household unless we believe, and keep on believing, right to the end.

This is obvious, if we are willing to think it through. Scripture consistently teaches that all saved people are not simply given a new standing in God's sight; they are also given a new nature and totally changed inside. Those whom God changes, he changes for ever. If someone claims to be a believer, but it later becomes obvious that their life has not become more holy, or that their faith is merely a temporary thing, it is because they are a not a true Christian at all.

There is a vast difference between what people call 'eternal security' and the scriptural teaching usually called 'the final perseverance of the saints'. Those who hold to 'eternal security' generally give the impression that anyone who claims to have received Christ must be regarded as a genuine believer. They are safe for time and for eternity, even if they later 'backslide' and never walk openly with the Lord again. They may miss out on God's blessing in this life, but they can never be lost.

'The final perseverance of the saints', which is especially emphasised in this Epistle to the Hebrews, looks at things very differently indeed. It is true that genuine believers have many ups and downs, and that not one of them is perfect in this life. They may even go very far away from the Lord, just as Peter did when he denied him. But they cannot stay away. They have been transformed inside, and their new nature constantly reveals that it is there. They return to the Lord, grow in spiritual strength and understanding, and never turn their back on Christ irretrievably.

If, having professed Christ, a person then leaves him for ever, it will be because their profession of faith was never genuine. They were never divinely changed. The only certain guarantee that you are a child of God is that you go on, and on, and on in the faith, despite your failings. If you show no signs of holiness or, worse, if you walk out on the Lord Jesus Christ, you will be lost.

It is important for us to be clear about this. If we are not, we will never be able to follow the third section of the passage we are currently studying. It is to that section that we now come.

(iii.) *Warning* (3:7-4:1)

It is obvious what the apostle's warning is going to be. He is going to tell the Hebrews (and us!) that if they do not go on and on in the faith, and do so until the very end, it will be because they do not belong to Christ. They will therefore be lost.

To do this he refers to Psalm 95:7-11, which is quoted in verses 7-11 of our chapter. This teaches that entry into the Promised Land was conditioned upon obedience. The fact that the generation who came out of Egypt perished in the wilderness was no accident. Out in the desert they contested God's authority and rebelled against him; they therefore perished there.

These people had experienced a marvellous and supernatural deliverance from their slavery in Egypt. They had received wonderful revelation at Sinai. God was providing for their needs on a daily basis, and they were witnesses of extraordinary miracles. They could say and sing, 'We are on the way to Canaan . . . God has acted for us . . . we have experienced a wonderful change . . .' But they never entered the Promised Land! Every one of them perished in the desert, just as God had threatened.

With this in mind, let us now take up the apostle's argument from verse 12:

3:12: 'Beware! Beware, lest the same thing happens to you; lest you fall into similar wilful neglect and disobedience; lest the same evil unbelief and obstinacy take hold of your heart—and you depart from the living God!'

3:13: 'The way to prevent this happening is by daily exhortation. Sin is deceitful; it is so easy to become hard-hearted. Therefore you must all keep encouraging and lecturing each other to go on, and on, and on.'

3:14: 'For we benefit from what Christ has done *only* as long as we continue as we began, *only* as long as we hold on.'

3:15: 'Perseverance is not something to think about tomorrow, but today, and every day, as the Psalm stresses. Do not close your heart to anything that God has said. Do not resist, rebel or grumble. Do not slacken off in holy disciplines. 'Today' is the keyword in the Christian life.

'Apostasy has happened in the past. On every occasion it be-gan "one day". So live this one day well. Concentrate on being the Christian you should be—not tomorrow—not only during the exciting times of great conferences, or summer beach missions and special events—but *today—here!*'

3:16: 'How was it with ancient Israel? They heard what God had to say, but they did not like what they heard. They murmured, complained, and rebelled. This was the general pattern, despite the two exceptions of Caleb and Joshua. The whole nation rebelled against God, sought alternative leadership, expressed dissatis-faction with his kind and miraculous provisions and, at one time or another, made plans to return to Egypt.'

3:17: 'It was with *those* people that God was grieved, angry, and vexed for forty years. It was the corpses of *those* people that, without exception, fell in the wilderness.'

3:18-19: 'It was to *those* disobedient and unbelieving people that he pledged that they would not enter into his promised rest in Canaan.

And they did not!'

4:1: 'So then, fear! Fear! There is a promised rest waiting for every believer. Heaven is a fact. It is the true home of each one of the Lord's people. So fear, lest *any of you* are apparently on the journey, but do not finally make it. The peril of apostasy is not theoretical; it is real!'

2. *Application*

Without any doubt, the passage has already spoken right into our hearts. It has made its own application. For the sake of our own spiritual welfare, let us repeat the application and make it even clearer. So little is said about apostasy today, and yet, as we have seen, it is a real danger. Where the subject is mentioned, it is surrounded with misunderstanding. More needs to be said. The verse numbers that follow all refer to the passage we have just studied.

(i.) *Apostasy: what it is*

Negatively, it is not holding fast to Christ and his gospel until the very end (3:6, 14). Positively, it is departing from the living God (3:12). The result is that the person concerned is no longer recognised as belonging to Christ (3:6b, 14) and fails to enter the rest that is promised to all who belong to Christ (4:1).

Apostasy, then, is something which happens *only* to those who appear to be true believers. This is what makes it such a solemn subject. Sadly, all of us know of people who have appeared to be outstanding Christians, but who have eventually ceased to make any Christian profession and have died in that state. It is important for us to remember, however, that the teaching of our passage is no longer applied to them, but to *us!*

(ii.) *Apostasy: how it happens*

It does not happen to all professing believers. 3:16 gives the impression that it does, but that clearly cannot be the case. Moses came out of Egypt, did he not? He did not enter into Canaan. But the passage is obviously not intending to classify him as one of the apostates. We know from the Old Testament Scriptures that Caleb and Joshua were also exceptions. The point of verse 16 is to underline what a widespread problem it is.

Apostasy starts in the heart, that is, in the affections and thoughts, in the inner person (3:8, 10b, 12, 15). The first thing that happens is that the person's heart becomes hard towards God's demands; it refuses to receive them (3:8, 13, 15) because, frankly, sin looks more attractive (3:13b).

Provocation follows—murmuring, dissatisfaction, complaining, and rebelling (3:8, 16). This leads to sinning, that is, the actual *doing* of what is forbidden, not unwillingly (as with a true believer in *Rom.* 7:13-25) but with active desire (3:17).

This leads to what our English version calls 'unbelief' (3:12, 18). The Greek word used here conveys the idea of obstinate rebellion and disobedience *caused* by unbelief. Where this is found, the final departure from the Lord has taken place. All that now remains are the threats of God (3:10-11, 18-19; 4:1) which, as we know, are not empty threats.

(iii.) *Apostasy: how it is prevented*

It is prevented, first of all, by realising that no professing believer will enter heaven unless he perseveres in the faith until the very end. This may not fit neatly into your particular understanding of theology, but it is the truth (3:6b, 14).

All of us who profess to follow Christ must realise that we are not exempt from apostatising. The apostle's use of the word 'any' underlines this (3:12-13; 4:1). Every one of us is to fear (4:1). We may believe that we are on the way to heaven, but it is possible that we may not get there.

To continue persevering in the faith, it is essential that we should join a fellowship of Christian believers. 3:13 clearly implies that this is necessary. Within that fellowship we are to get close to others, and we are to allow them to get close to us. We are to constantly encourage and admonish them to go on and on in the things of God, and they are to do the same to us. We are not called to 'stand on our own two feet'. Our hearts are too deceitful for that. Others may spot things in our beliefs and lives that need correction. We are to put ourselves in a position where they can notice these things, and we are to humbly receive what they say to us, and to act on it.

But even that is not enough. Above everything else we are to 'consider the apostle and high priest of our confession, Christ Jesus' (3:1). Those who constantly have Christ in their thoughts, and whose hearts go out to him in adoration, thankfulness, love and obedience, are always perfectly safe. This is the main lesson of the Epistle to the Hebrews.

God has not made it hard for us to persevere. If we keep the file-leader in our sights, follow him and keep close to him, we will arrive safely in heaven and enjoy the eternal rest that he has promised us.

> Walk thou with Him; that way is light,
> All other pathways end in night:
> Walk thou with Him; that way is rest,
> All other pathways are unblest.[2]

6

THE PROMISED REST

PLEASE READ HEBREWS 4:2-16

The Promised Rest

The apostle has been writing very bluntly about apostasy, knowing full well that his teaching would raise all sorts of questions in people's minds. Readers today ask the same questions, even if they do not always express them. In chapter 4 the apostle does not repeat the questions, but he does give the answers. Let us see how he does it.

1. Isn't the Reason the Israelites Apostatised the Fact that They Did Not Have the Advantages that We Have? (4:2)

The apostle's answer is 'No!' We have been 'gospelled' (as the apostle puts it in Greek) and so had they. In other words, both we and they have received messages from God—messages of good news, salvation and hope.

The trouble with the Israelites is not that they had *not* heard the word. They heard it all right, but it did not do them any good. And why was that? It is because of the way that they received it. They did not combine their hearing with faith. They did not receive the message for what it is, namely, the word of God. They trifled with it. They did not take it seriously. They did not believe it, they did not act upon it in holy fear; in fact, they resisted it, as we have now seen several times.

That, ultimately, is the difference between apostasy and persever-ance. Those who depart from the faith do so because they do not take God's Word seriously. Those who persevere do so because they continue to receive God's Word and to act upon it.

This teaching is very searching. When I hear the Bible preached, what happens to me? Do I treat the message as just one more ser-mon? Or do I take it to heart as the Word of God? And how about the verse we have just looked at? Do I just see it as the next verse to be studied, or is it a divine message to be taken seriously? The person who receives God's Word humbly, quietly and with awe is eternally safe, but who can tell the danger to which we expose ourselves if we treat the Word of God in the same way as we treat the word of men!

2. When the Israelites Failed To Enter the Promised Rest of Canaan, Didn't the Promises about Rest Expire? (4:3-11)

Some people find it hard to follow the apostle's train of thought at this point. In fact it is quite straightforward, as we shall now see.

The Scriptures often speak of God's 'rest'—something which God himself enjoys and wants his people to enter into. God rested after the sixth day of creation, but this fact does not exhaust all that is meant by the term. We know this because, long after creation was finished, he spoke through Moses of a rest he wanted Israel to experience. He pictured this rest by referring to Canaan.

But even when Israel, led by Joshua, entered Canaan, they did not actually experience the promised rest. We know this because Psalm 95 dates from a time long after their entry into Canaan. Written at the time of David, it continues to promise rest and urges that 'today' they should not harden their hearts, lest they fail to enter into it.

The main points of the argument of 4:3-11 are thus as follows:

• 'Following the six days of creation, the seventh day was a rest (3b-4).

• 'Such a rest was promised to Israel, but they did not enter into it. This was because of their disobedience (4:3, 5-6).

• 'The rest, however, continued to be promised to them, and they were urged to experience it (4:7).

• 'If Joshua had managed to get them into that rest, such a continuing promise of it could not have been made (4:8).

• 'There is, then, *still* a promised rest for the people of God to enter into (4:9).

• 'It is "a Sabbath rest" (as the Greek puts it), that is, a rest from toil and labour, but not a rest of inactivity (4:10). It is the blissful and perfect enjoyment of God. Such a rest remains and is waiting for us to experience it! It is not a state of striving to please God, but of relaxing and of finding all our pleasure in him. Adam, before he fell, must have experienced some taste of this, and every Sabbath day was also intended to convey some idea of it.

• 'But we are not there yet! So, take all steps necessary to make sure that you get there lest, like Israel, your disobedience keeps you out of it' (4:11).

In the Bible there are such things as 'types', that is, models or pictures of spiritual realities. The seventh day following creation is a type of heaven. So is the Sabbath day, so is Canaan, and so is the peace of conscience that the believer experiences after coming to Christ. A type represents a spiritual reality, but it is *not* that reality. Heaven itself is something that we have not entered into—yet!

It is time to think more about heaven. As Christians we escape the City of Destruction by the way of the cross. As we journey towards it, we sometimes get glimpses of the Celestial City. We are not there yet. But if we keep walking, if we keep on going on, we will get there! Nothing will keep us out except unbelief, that is, resistance to God's Word, leading us eventually to walk out on Christ.

Think of it—a few more years, or even less, and we shall be there! Who can put into words what that will mean? Today, then, is not a day to treat sin sympathetically. It is, rather, a day to pay serious attention to God's Word; to make every effort necessary to be a stronger, better and wiser Christian; and to be sure of arriving. When we hear all the trumpets sound for us on the other side, we will know that it has all been worth it. And so we shall be for ever with the Lord!

3. You Have Said a Good Deal about Those who Appear To Be on the Way to Canaan, but Never Get There. How Can I Know Whether I Am Such a Person or Not? (4:12-13)

The answer to that is to expose yourself to the Word of God (4:12). It is not a dead book, but very much alive. It does not leave you unaffected, because it is active and powerful. It pricks, wounds, cuts, and slays more effectively than the finest and sharpest sword. It gets right in where nothing else can. It separates what *cannot* be separated!

It shows you what you are really like in your innermost being. It deals with your thoughts, and even with your intentions. Yes, it is by his Word that God deals with people (4:13). All that we are is an open book to him. Nothing is hidden from his gaze and, by his Word, he reveals to us what he sees. God is the one with whom we have to deal, and by his Word he brings us to realise how completely he reads us. By his Word we are brought to see what he has seen all along.

Many people think that they are on the way to Canaan. The illusion persists because they never expose themselves to God's Word. If they were to attentively listen to the Scriptures, their illusion would be shattered. At that point they would either be filled with furious anger, or would be broken in repentance.

On the other hand, there are true Christians who enjoy assurance of salvation, but then lose it. In very many cases, this is because they neglect serious listening to the Scriptures. They thus fail to regularly see the marks of a true believer that are found there, and to see themselves as people who have those marks. The comfort of full assurance thus leaves them.

There is no coming to faith without the Word, and there is no continuing in the faith without the Word. Those who neglect the Scriptures cannot grow in grace and knowledge and cannot know intimacy with the Lord. It is by his Word that he does what he does in his creatures.

4. But, with All My Heart, I Want To Keep Going Right to the End. What Must I Do? (4:14-16)

You must realise that there is someone who has been among us, but who is now experiencing the promised rest (4:14). If you are going to get help from anywhere, you must get it from him. He has ascended beyond the physical heavens and, in God's own presence, he represents all believers as their great high priest. He is the eternal Son of God, and yet he still carries his human name of Jesus. He is for us, and not against us. There is no need for any of us to loosen our grip on what we have been brought to believe and confess.

Take your eyes of yourself and fix them on him (4:15). Do not think of him as unfeeling; everything you are facing, he has already faced. He understands completely and sympathises with your weakness. See him as powerful and as perfectly qualified to help you; he has been exactly where you are, yet was never tainted in any way by any sort of sin. You do not need to look anywhere else!

He is the Son of God, so his throne is a throne of glory. But he is also the Son of Man, and his throne is a throne of grace (4:16). He is generous in spirit and overflowing with kindness. Come, and keep on coming, to this throne. You will find mercy for every detail of the mess you have made. You will find grace and supernatural strengthening in your time of need. There is no need to stand on ceremony. There is nothing to do but to come to him and to call on him.

In Christ there is pardon, welcome, sympathy, and help. By all means contemplate him, but do not forget to come to him. Do it again and again, and again and again. Do not hide your weakness from him; he is willing to help. He knows all the mistakes you have made and continue to make. He knows how often you will need to come back. He knows that you cannot pray as you ought. He knows that even your holiest moment is polluted by sin. He knows that even the strongest faith is mixed with unbelief—and yet the invitation to come remains open. We are invited to come boldly. Mercy may still be found. Grace is still available.

Do you now see the secret of persevering? It is the old way of loving the Bible and coming to the Lord in prayer. There is no need to look for a spectacular secret, because there isn't one. We need to keep on coming to Christ in his Word and by prayer, publicly, privately, and as couples and families. No one who is close to Christ can fail to come to the place where he is—in heaven.

7

CHRIST'S HIGH PRIESTHOOD

PLEASE READ HEBREWS 5:1-10

Having bluntly warned his hearers about the peril of apostasy, the apostle has shown them (and us), how to persevere. We are to expose ourselves to the Word of God and to look away to the Lord Jesus Christ, coming constantly to him in the way described at the end of chapter 4.

The mention of Jesus as 'a great high priest' would have raised the eyebrows of the original readers. They will have asked, 'How can you refer to Jesus as a high priest. This is what you did in 2:17 and 3:1, and here you are doing it again. In what way is Jesus a high priest, and how is he qualified for such a task?'

The apostle now sets himself to answer questions of this sort and, in doing so, he comes to the very core and centre of his letter. The subject of the high-priestly ministry of Christ is the most dominant feature of the Epistle to the Hebrews, and it must have had a profound effect on the first readers. In Judaism the office of high priest was the highest religious office of all. Jews spoke with great reverence of the first high priest, Aaron; and one of the great attractions drawing these Hebrew Christians back to what they had left was the continuing high-priestly ministry going on in Jerusalem.

What the apostle will now do is this: he will show that the Lord Jesus Christ is indeed a high priest and that there is therefore no need to return to Judaism in order to have one. Indeed, he is a greater high priest than any who ever existed in Judaism, Aaron included. To turn from him to a Jewish high priest is, once more, to turn from the greater to the lesser.

Now there is no essential difference between a priest and a high priest; the second is just an exalted version of the first. The apostle will therefore begin his discussion by outlining what qualifications are essential for a man to be a priest. This he does in verses 1-4. He will then show how the Lord Jesus Christ meets these requirements perfectly. This he does in verses 5-10.

1. The qualifications essential for a man to be a priest (5:1-4)

There are two essential qualifications for a man to be a priest, of which the first is spelled out in verses 1-3:

5:1: Since his task is to represent man to God (whereas that of a prophet is to represent God to man), he must himself be a man. He is taken from among men, and set apart from them in order to act for them. He gives himself to ministering to God on man's behalf, principally by presenting gifts and offering sacrifices for sins.

5:2: Being a man, he can understand human weakness, for he himself is weak. This means that he can tenderly help those who are ignorant, or who are wandering spiritually. His sympathy is real, because he is prone to all the same problems. It is important to note that the priest does not only represent men and women to God, but he pastors them as well.

5:3: Yes, he too is a sinner, just like those for whom he acts. So, when he offers sacrifices for sins, he has to offer sacrifices for himself as well as others. So the first qualification for priesthood is plain: the humanity of the priest is essential to his office.

With this made clear, the apostle spells out the second essential qualification in verse 4.

5:4: No man, in and of himself, can simply decide that he is going to be a priest. He is representing man, so he must be a man. But he is representing him to *God,* so he must be acceptable to God, and therefore appointed by him. That is how Aaron became a priest; he did not seek the office, nor did he deserve it, but God called him into it. Others who sought to take to themselves the priestly office, such as, for example, the sons of Korah (*Num.* 16:1-40), met with the fierce anger and judgement of God.

These are the two qualifications essential for any priest—he must be taken from among men, and he must be chosen by God. Now does Jesus meet these requirements? Is the apostle justified in calling *him* a 'high priest'? We will now be shown that he meets both qualifications perfectly. It is interesting to note that the writer deals with the second qualification first (5:5-6), before moving on to stress the first qualification (5:7-8). Why does he do this? It is because Christ was appointed by God to do this work long *before* he became a man, which was certainly not true of the Levitical priests.

2. Christ perfectly meets these qualifications (5:5-10)

5:5-6: Christ did not take this glorious office to himself. He was appointed to it by God. It was God who spoke to him the words of eternal generation[1] found in Psalm 2:7, and it was God who appointed him as a priest, as expressed in the words of Psalm 110:4. But it was not to the Levitical priesthood that he was appointed. In eternity, such a priesthood did not exist. He was appointed 'a priest for ever according to the order of Melchizedek'. The apostle does not explain here precisely what that means, although he will do so later. What is clear is that it is an eternal priesthood, and that Christ has been a priest of that order for as long as he has been God the Son—which is from all eternity. He therefore clearly fulfils the second requirement of a priest, that is, that he should be appointed by God.

5:7-8: But how about the first qualification, that is, that he must be taken from among men? He fulfils this requirement too. He had a human experience of learning and limitations. The eternal Son of God became a man, and we can talk about 'the days of his flesh'! It was during this time that he went through the awful experience of Gethsemane, sweating as it were great drops of blood (*Luke* 22:44) and praying to be saved 'out of death' (as it is in the Greek). His prayer was answered. He was saved 'out of death'! God raised him from the dead in the power of an endless life (*Heb.* 7:16). His piety and godly fear secured for him a hearing.

Yes, the eternal Son of God went through that experience as a man, and by it 'he learned obedience' in a way that he would never have learned it otherwise. What the apostle is teaching is that the horror of Calvary's cross tested Christ's obedience to the limit. He is not a person who was able to continue in mere innocence, simply because he never went through any trials. His obedience as a Son remained unspoiled and unblemished, even though it meant he had to go through the worst suffering that the universe has ever seen.

Our Lord was a man among men—a *perfect* man among men. His obedience was tried and tested, but he fleshed out perfection at every step of his life. He went through trials that he would never have faced if he had not become incarnate. As the eternal Son of God, he continued to be what he always was. But he became what he had never been before—a man; and there was never a moment when he was anything less than a perfect man.

5:9-10: So what does it mean, then, when it says in verse 9 that Christ was 'perfected'? It is not a reference to moral perfection. He had that already. It means that he became ripe or mature, perfectly fitted and suited for his work as high priest; and, because of this fitness and suitability, he became to all who obey him the author of eternal salvation.

The eternal Son of God became a man and remains a man. He is the one eternally appointed by God to be 'a priest for ever according to the order of Melchizedek'. There is a man who is an eternal priest!

Many men in history have been priests for a time. As we have seen, all of them, without exception, were sinners. But there *is* somebody who *became* a man, is a man, and is a *perfect* man, who nonetheless in eternity was appointed to an eternal priesthood. There is no one else like that, nor has there ever been. Christ's priesthood is unique, which is why it could be described as it was in 4:14-16.

Why would anyone want to turn from that to the lesser priesthood of Judaism? Could anything be more foolish than to turn from such greatness to something so obviously poor in comparison? Our Lord Jesus Christ is wonderfully great both in his person (who he is) and his work (what he has done, and is doing). Everything about him, and everything connected to him, is vast and glorious and awesome. Why walk from the sunshine into the shadows?

8

A REBUKE AND
AN EXHORTATION

PLEASE READ HEBREWS 5:11-6:3

The Hebrews to whom this epistle is addressed are Jews who have become Christians, but who are now seriously thinking of giving everything up and of going back to Judaism. The apostle has bluntly warned them that if they do not go on and on in the Christian life, to the very end, they will be lost and will perish in outer darkness. He has not minced his words in speaking to them of the peril of apostasy and has urged them to expose themselves to God's Word, and to keep looking to the Lord Jesus Christ, coming to him as their high priest.

In the verses leading up to our present passage, he has explained how it is possible to speak of Jesus as a priest, and has twice mentioned that he is a priest 'according to the order of Melchizedek'. His mention of this fact now leads him to give the Hebrews a stern rebuke.

1. A rebuke (5:11-14)

The apostle knows very well the mindset of the people to whom he is writing, and so, in mentioning that Christ is a priest according to the order of Melchizedek, a thought crosses his mind. He would like to say a lot more about this subject, but what is the point? The Hebrews will not understand it (11a).

The truth he has mentioned is one of the deeper truths of the Christian faith, and it is difficult to explain. The Hebrews, however, are 'dull of hearing' (11b). In spiritual matters, they are not very quick on the uptake. They are slow to learn. The truth he would like to spend time speaking about is well beyond their capacity to understand.

> 5:12: 'At this stage in your Christian life you ought to be teachers of the Christian faith. Instead of that, what has happened? You are still in the elementary class, needing others to instruct you in the very basics of the Christian faith.
>
> 'You are like children who have been born a long time, but who are still unable to feed on anything but milk. You cannot yet take solid food. You cannot get your teeth into anything of substance. You are no more advanced spiritually than when you were first born again.'

> 5:13: 'To be limited to milk is to remain a baby when, by this time, you should have grown up. You are "unskilled in the word of right-eousness"; in other words, you cannot handle it, because you are not accustomed to it. You do not know your way round the Word; you do not know how to use it. No wonder that you cannot grasp what it means for Christ to be "a priest for ever according to the order of Melchizedek!"'

> 5:14: 'Only mature believers can take solid food. And how do they get into that condition? It is "by reason of use"—they get used to chewing and digesting solid food. And what is the sign that some-one has arrived at maturity? They "have their senses exercised to discern both good and evil"; they can tell truth from error, and right behaviour from wrong.'

How valuable these four verses are to us! They underline the importance of going on and on, and show us how to know whether we are doing so. They tell us how to measure whether we are mak-ing spiritual progress or not.

We have to keep two pictures in mind; that of a baby growing up, and that of a school. What is your place in the school, that of an infant being taught the most basic things of all, or that of a teacher?

Are there truths that seem impossibly difficult for you to understand? They are like meat that you chew and chew, but you can never manage to swallow. Is that how the truth of Christ as a priest for ever after the order of Melchizedek appears? And are there parts of the Bible that are still strange to you? You are unaccustomed to them, and can make neither head nor tail of them.

Or is your situation completely different? Do you now, because of your constant use of Scripture, understand much more clearly what is right and what is wrong? Do you find that it is not difficult for you to distinguish truth from error? Gone are the days when you sometimes confused the two.

Each of us needs to ask how we measure up. Those who have been converted recently should not be troubled if they do badly. The apostle's remarks are not addressed to them, but to those who have been Christians for some time.

If we can see that we have made progress, we should be filled with thankfulness. Nonetheless, we should remember that we still have further to go. We are not yet as holy on earth as it is possible for a saved sinner to be.

A much greater peril, however, is that of discovering that we have made little or no progress. We are spiritually static. This is as much a tragedy as that of a baby several years old who has not developed at all since birth. How heart breaking! And how dangerous! Anyone in that condition must do something, and must do it right away. Chapter 6 will bluntly warn all such people about staying as they are. However, before it does so, the apostle pleads with his readers by means of an exhortation.

2. An exhortation (6:1-3)

This paragraph urges us not to be content with feeding solely on milk, but to progress to solid food; not to be content with remaining in the infants' class, but to progress up the school until at last we become teachers.

The 'leaving' of verse 1 does not mean 'forget' but, rather, 'leave behind and go further'. Children need to learn their multiplication tables by heart. When they have done so, it is not the end of their mathematical study. They are not to stop where they are, but to use their knowledge to help them in their future learning.

No Christian should be content to remain a doctrinal novice. They should not be satisfied that they know only a little, namely the basics. Their ambition must be to understand more. *This* is the way to maturity, because all human behaviour is governed by what a person believes. In any case, the obedient believer who knows very little of God's ways will not be a patch on the obedient believer who knows God's ways well. The way to maturity is the way of the mind. It is by *knowing* that we grow.

How different this is from some views that are popular in many Bible-believing churches at the moment! The idea has somehow grown up that it is possible to make progress in the Christian life, even if you by-pass the mind completely. Countless professing Christians believe that it is by something 'happening' to you that you grow. If something special or dramatic 'happens' when Christians are together, it is considered to be 'a great meeting'. Euphoria, enthusiastic singing, weeping and prostration are therefore often welcomed without further thought, while preachers ascend the platform longing for something to 'happen' during the sermon.

On the strength of this passage, we must disassociate ourselves completely from such an approach to the Christian life. All spiritual progress, without exception, is linked to the understanding. The preacher should go on to the platform saying to himself, 'Edification,

edification, edification!' A 'great meeting' is not one where everyone feels wonderful, or where something special happens, but where our minds are stretched to know something of God's Word that we did not know before. Progress takes place when something takes place in the mind. True emotion will follow, although that subject is beyond the scope of this present passage.

The apostle's exhortation, then, is that we should not be content to keep going over and over the fundamentals, but that we should go beyond that, on to 'perfection', that is, to spiritual maturity. Let us do that! And we will, God willing! (verse 3).

But, of course, no one can build on the fundamental truths unless they know what they are. So the apostle gives us this information in verses 1b-2. He mentions six basic doctrines. These are grouped into three pairs. The first pair deals with salvation, the second with ordinances, and the third with the final state.

The person who knows and understands only *this* much, is still a baby living on milk. It is time to look at the three pairs closely and carefully. Some readers will see that they do not even have a grasp of these things! If so, it is because they are not even on the milk; they are only just about alive. They are not in the kindergarten, and they are not even in the school playground!

The immature believer is the one who only understands this much. The progressing Christian is the one who has a firm grasp of these things and who is now absorbing truth which is more difficult and profound. If you have only got these six doctrines clear in your mind, you have done no more than lay the foundation of your Christian life. Do not be happy with that—build something on it! But if you are not clear about these six doctrines, then you have not even laid a foundation, and everything you try to build in the future will surely collapse.

Let us look at the first pair, namely, 'repentance from dead works and . . . faith towards God' (verse 1b). Are you clear how the

Christian life begins? It begins by the painful realisation that we have never pleased God in any way at all. We therefore make up our mind to turn our back on all that we have lived for in the past. In doing this, we turn towards God. We entrust ourselves to him, asking him to forgive us and to save us. We believe that he will do so, because of all that he has done by sending the Saviour to live for sinners, to die for sinners, and to live for ever to receive sinners and bring them to him.

Now let us look at the final pair, namely, the 'resurrection of the dead and . . . eternal judgement' (verse 2b). Are you clear about where the Christian life leads to? It leads to the day when we will be raised from the dead and even physically will be like Christ. At the final judgement God will openly acknowledge that we belong to him and, despite our guilt, but because of what Christ has done for us, he will announce that we are guiltless in his sight. With our public acquittal ringing in our ears, we will proceed to the holiness and happiness of heaven, where we will fully enjoy God through-out eternity

Now let us look at the central pair, namely, 'the doctrine of baptisms (and) of laying on of hands' (verse 2a). What, exactly, is the apostle talking about? Everyone who studies the Bible agrees that this is a difficult phrase to interpret. This is not encouraging. The apostle is talking about an 'elementary principle' of the Christian life (verse 1); but if we cannot be sure what it is, how can we possibly know whether we have properly laid our spiritual foundation or not?

It is not that difficult. When all has been said and done, there are only two interpretations which are worth considering. The first one believes that by 'baptisms' the apostle is referring to the various ceremonial washings that took place in Old Testament days. They only cleansed the body, whereas repentance is how the heart is cleansed. 'Laying on of hands' was done on an animal that was about to take the sinner's place as a sacrifice or scapegoat. By faith, the worshipper saw his sins transferred to a substitute, knowing that a better sacrifice (the promised Christ) would one day have to come to truly take the sinner's place. The apostle is thus referring to Old Testament pictures of the repentance and faith which he has just mentioned, and which are found in every believer's heart in every age.

For myself, I think that that interpretation is plausible. But it does not convince me because, if it is true, it is simply a round-about repetition of what has just been said. For myself, I would stress that the apostle is talking about spiritual basics and mentioning three pairs of fundamental truths. The first pair deals with how the Christian life begins. The third pair deals with where the Christian life leads. The middle pair then must deal with what lies in between, that is, our day to day Christian life. That is the way it seems to me.

'Baptisms' is in the plural. 1 Corinthians 12:13 tells us that although we Christians come from all sorts of different backgrounds, we have all had one common uniting experience; we have been baptised in the Holy Spirit, and have been initiated into the spiritual life. It is this experience that makes us members of Jesus Christ's church. By the baptism of the Spirit we become organs in the body of which Christ is the Head. The outward and visible sign of this is baptism in water. The inward baptism and the outward baptism are thus, in fact, one baptism, so as Christians we have 'one Lord, one faith, one baptism' (*Eph.* 4:5). Starting by repenting and believing, and ending up at the resurrection and eternal judgement, we live the whole of our Christian life in between in the context of the church. This is a basic truth.

What then is the 'laying on of hands' mentioned in verse 2? In New Testament days some people had hands laid on them on the day of their conversion, but they were few. It is more likely that this is a reference to the laying on of hands that took place when deacons or elders were appointed, or when men were set apart for church planting or similar ministries (*Acts* 6:6; 13:3; *1 Tim.* 4:14; 5:22; *2 Tim.* 1:6). Although Christ is the only Head of his church, it is his will that each local expression of his church should be led by godly men whom he has set apart for the purpose. Local churches publicly recognise such men by setting them apart formally by the laying on of hands. It is a basic tenet of the Christian faith that the Christian life is lived in the context of local churches whose submission to Christ is ensured by godly men whom he has chosen. The babe in Christ who does not understand this will always remain immature.

* * * * *

Speaking for myself, I find this passage to be immensely challenging. The apostle has clearly spelled out the issues—we go on and on, and are saved; or we do not go on, and are lost. The way for me to discover whether I am making progress is to ask myself whether I have a growing understanding of God's Word.

I do not believe that the apostle is saying that only theological 'egg-heads' are to be considered to be growing. A simple intellectual grasp of divine truth is nothing. A growing understanding of God's Word will always (without any exceptions) reveal itself in a transformed life. A person who really gets hold of what God says will be increasingly different in the way they think, the way they speak, and the way that they behave. Not only so, but in the whole of their life between conversion and heaven they will be committed to, and active in, a local church whose submission to Christ is guaranteed by godly men whom he has set apart for the purpose.

Therefore, leaving the discussion of the elementary principles of Christ, let us go on to perfection . . . and this we will do, if God permits.

9

A TERRIFYING WARNING

PLEASE READ HEBREWS 6:4-8

The apostle has warned the wandering Hebrews about the peril of apostasy and has urged them to progress to spiritual maturity. He has talked to them very frankly indeed. Because there is so much at stake, he is now going to be even blunter. The verses before us contain a terrifying warning, and it is important for our own spiritual good that we do not water it down. We will understand it well enough if we take four steps.

1. To understand this passage we must keep in mind the parable of the sower

The Parable of the Sower is found in Matthew 13:1-23, Mark 4:1-20, and Luke 8:1-15. Could I ask you at this point to read it again, as it is in Mark's Gospel?

Everyone agrees that Hebrews 6:4-8 is hard to understand. We believe, however, that Scripture explains Scripture; if we know the whole, we will better understand the parts. Could any part be more important than the teaching that our Lord gave during his earthly ministry? And is not most of this made up of parables? (*Mark* 4:33-34). And has not our Lord made clear that no parable is more important than this one? (*Mark* 4:13).

The Parable of the Sower teaches us that whenever God's Word is taught, it meets with different responses. First of all, there are those who hear it, but on whom it has no effect at all (*Mark* 4:14-15). Secondly, there are those who receive it with immediate enthusiasm, but who, quite quickly, have nothing more to do with it. This is because they discover that it costs something to go God's way (*Mark* 4:16-17).

Then, thirdly, there are those who receive the Word and it has a lasting effect on them (*Mark* 4:18-19). The seed germinates, the shoots grow strongly upwards, and everything seems fine. But, at the same time, something else is growing. Eventually the 'something else' becomes the stronger, and it strangles the life out of the emerging plant. Just at the moment it is about to burst into fruit, it withers away. What looked so promising comes to nothing; 'the cares of this world, the deceitfulness of riches, and the desires for other things entering in, choke the word, and it becomes unfruitful' (*Mark* 4:19).

Finally, there are those who receive the Word and are changed for ever (*Mark* 4:20). The seed germinates, grows, bears fruit and endures. In some cases the seed multiplies itself thirtyfold; the fruit of the Spirit is evident and there is a change of character. In other cases the fruit is sixtyfold; the Christ-like character of the person is even more obvious. And in some cases, the fruit is one hundredfold; there are such people as saintly saints!

This is the parable that we need to bear in mind as we study Hebrews 6:4-8, especially as there are obvious parallels with it in verses 7-8.

2. In the parable the third and fourth responses are, for a considerable period, indistinguishable—and can be described in identical terms

In looking at the third and fourth groups mentioned in the parable, we can ask a number of questions. Have the birds stolen the seed? Have the plants only put down shallow roots? Do they grow quickly? When the sun comes out, do they wither away? For both these groups, the answer to all these questions is 'No'.

In both cases the roots go down and the shoots grow up. The stalks reach towards the sky and the heads begin to appear. The ears take shape and look very promising. It is only at this point that any difference between the two sorts of plant becomes apparent. Up until then we can describe them in identical terms.

With all this clear in our minds, let us now look at verses 4-5 of our passage and, at the same time, imagine two men called John and Jack. John has been 'enlightened'; he has had a definite spiritual experience which has caused him to see the truth of the gospel. He has 'tasted the heavenly gift'; that is, he knows something of the benefits and blessings of the gospel. He has had a genuine experience of the Holy Spirit; you can describe him as a 'partaker of the Holy Spirit' because he is not a stranger to the Holy Spirit's work. For John, God's Word is 'good'; he enjoys hearing it preached and relishes reading it. Invisible and eternal things grip him; he has tasted 'the powers of the age to come'. In short, John is a real believer (as we shall see as we proceed) and verses 4-5 describe him accurately.

Now let us talk about Jack. He, too, has been 'enlightened'; he has had a definite spiritual experience which has caused him to see the truth of the gospel. He has 'tasted the heavenly gift'; that is, he knows something of the benefits and blessings of the gospel. He has had a genuine experience of the Holy Spirit; you can describe him as 'a partaker of the Holy Spirit' because he is not a stranger to the Holy Spirit's work. For Jack, God's Word is 'good'; he enjoys hearing it preached and relishes reading it. Invisible and eternal things grip him; he has tasted 'the powers of the age to come'. Verses 4-5 certainly describe him accurately.

However, although we cannot see it as we look at him, Jack is later going to apostatise and be lost. Just like in the Parable of the

Sower, we can at the moment describe him and John in the same terms; for the time being the two of them are indistinguishable. For a considerable period the words that we use to describe one will exactly fit the other. At this point there is no discernible difference between the true believer and the eventual apostate.

3. The true believer and the apostate become distinguishable eventually

The difference between them becomes clear over time. In the Parable of the Sower one plant goes on to bear fruit, thirtyfold, sixtyfold, or even one hundredfold. The other one looks promising for ages and comes to the point where everyone expects it to produce a great harvest. But it never gets there. The life is strangled out of it. The third piece of ground is, in the long term, unchanged. It is as barren and fruitless at the end as it was before the seed was sown there.

Let us go back to John. He experiences everything described in verses 4-5. But he does not fall away. In his spiritual life he goes on and on and on. He continues to expose himself to the Word of God and, through constant use, he becomes skilful in the word of righteousness (see 5:12-14). From a diet of milk he graduates to a diet of solid food; he proceeds from being taught to being a teacher. He continues to look all the time to Jesus Christ, his great high priest (see 4:14-16). When he fails, he comes to Christ for mercy; when in need, he comes to him for grace. In spiritual understanding and character, he never ceases to make progress; slowly but surely John is becoming a holy man.

John is rather like a field upon which the rain falls (verse 7)—the rain is God's Word and God's Spirit. The field produces the fruit which pleases and delights God. The Lord sees what is happening and smiles favourably on John who, by his permanently transformed life, is showing that he has a new nature. God is receiving something for his work in John's life, and, as a result, John enjoys his blessing. Despite his strong and sincere warnings to the Hebrews, the apostle is convinced that they are, in fact, like John (verse 9).

Jack stands out in sharp contrast to John, but not immediately. He too experiences everything that is listed in verses 4-5. His problem is that in addition to all this, other things are growing in his life. These eventually become bigger and end up strangling the Word. Jack's interest in that Word begins to wane. He does not expose himself to it in the way that he used to, because his appetite has been affected. His growing understanding slowly comes to a standstill; he loses all desire for solid food and, slowly, even for milk.

Despite all that he once knew and all that he has experienced, 'the cares of this world' finally become more important to Jack than the mercy and grace of Christ. 'The deceitfulness of riches' deceives him and 'the desires for other things' rule his life. But he is not the victim of an unfortunate accident; he has deliberately opted for these things. He has walked out on what he knows to be true, the power of which he has experienced. In the words of verse 6, he has chosen to 'fall away'.

Falling away is a deliberate act. It occurs when somebody, by a series of choices, walks away from an active Christian life, although they know full well who the Lord Jesus Christ is and what he has done. They take their eyes off him. In reality they treat him as an imposter and a deceiver, although they know differently, and so in their hearts they crucify him again (verse 6). They behave as if there is nothing good in Christ. The result is that they bring upon him public shame and contempt, because the watching world then sneers, 'Isn't he the man who claimed to follow Christ and urged us to do the same? Now look at him! In the end, Jesus Christ made no difference to him, did he? It doesn't look like there is anything in this Christianity after all.'

Jack, too, has received the 'rain' of the influences of God's Word and Spirit (verse 7). But at the end of the day there is no fruit there. There is no lasting sign of any work of God. All that can be found is a field of 'thorns and briars' (verse 8). What use is ground like that? It is 'rejected and near to being cursed'. The only thing to be done is to burn the whole field up.

John and Jack looked identical, and that is the way it was for ages. But they were not identical, as subsequent events proved. One was truly changed, because he was permanently changed. The other one experienced a real change, but eventually went back to what he was before. In fact he was even worse than he was before; the ground which was ready for planting ended up covered in thorns and briars.

Although correct doctrine is vital, the proof that someone is a genuine believer does not lie in the fact that they believe all the right things. Even the devil could sign up to the great confessions of the Reformation! And although spiritual experience is a fact, the proof that someone is a true believer does not lie in the fact that they have had such experiences. The Bible makes it clear that not every true experience of the Holy Spirit is a *saving* experience. The proof that someone is a true believer lies in the fact that their character has been permanently transformed. This is seen in their growing understanding of spiritual things, in their increasing Christlikeness, and in their persevering in the faith until the very end. It is important that we should be clear about all of this. So much is at stake. The fact is that true believers are eternally saved, and everybody else—whatever they may have appeared to be at times in their life—is lost.

4. This teaching leaves some points to be cleared up

(i.) *This passage is teaching that such people who walk out on the gospel can never be restored* (6:4a)

It is impossible (4a); that is what the apostle says, and there should be no debate about it. The starting point for the Christian life is repentance (verse 1) and they cannot come back there (verse 6a).

This is because they have committed blasphemy against the Holy Spirit, which is a sin that can never be forgiven (see *Mark* 3:28-30). In Mark 3:20-30 it was clear to all that our Lord had come from heaven; this was seen in his miracles, and particularly in his casting out of demons by the simple authority of his word. His enemies, however, attributed his power to the devil. What was clearly divine, they called diabolical; what was clearly light, they called darkness; what was clearly right, they called wrong. To them, holiness was evil. Such a condition is blasphemy against the Holy Spirit, and it is obvious that someone in that condition will never come to Christ to be saved, nor will they even want to. The blasphemy against the Holy Spirit can never be forgiven.

Apostates commit the same sin. They know that the gospel is true and have had the experiences of verses 4-5. But they walk out on it all. They treat the truth like falsehood and their experiences as if they had never happened. It is blasphemy against the Holy Spirit. It may not happen all at once, but, by a series of deliberate steps, this is where they get to.

Apostasy is not backsliding. Backsliders may go very far from the Lord and may remain there for a long time. Onlookers may even conclude that they are apostates. But they are not. The proof is that they come back to the Lord again. They never walk away from him permanently. At last they experience what no apostate can ever experience again—repentance (6a). They return boldly to the throne of grace, to obtain mercy and to find grace to help in time of need (4:16). And they find that despite their sins and failures, their great High Priest has lost none of his welcoming tenderness.

Apostasy is not spiritual immaturity. The Hebrews were spiritually immature. They were still on milk when they should have been feeding on solid food (5:12-14). They still needed to be taught, although by that time they should have been teachers. But they had not walked out on the faith, although it was in their minds to do so. This is why the apostle tells them that he does not believe them to be apostates (verse 9). His warning to them is nonetheless real, and not in any way hypothetical: if they do walk out on the faith, they will certainly be lost (verses 1-8).

The only certain sign you have of being a true Christian is that you go on and on and on in the faith. Not to go on is eventually to go back. Those who go back end up going out. There is no safe course except to go forward, which, with God's help, is an option for us all (verse 3). The apostle will come back to this point on several more occasions, and will continue to be as blunt as he is here. 'Pursue peace with all men', he will say, 'and holiness, without which no one will see the Lord: looking diligently lest anyone should fall short of the grace of God' (12:14). For those who deliberately fall away, he will hold out no hope; while the apostle John will tell us that we should not even feel bound to pray for them (*1 John* 5:16).

(ii.) *We must not think that the language of 6:4-5 is too strong to use of the unregenerate*

There is nothing said in verses 4-5 which cannot be said of the Israelites who came out of Egypt and then died in the desert. The apostle has already spoken about them at length in chapters 3 and

4. These men and women had true experiences of God which were not saving experiences—they were led by the pillar of fire and cloud, they walked on dry land across the Red Sea, they drank from the rock, ate the manna, fed on miraculously provided quails, and even heard the voice of God. But their characters were not changed; they died in unbelief and never experienced God's rest.

There is nothing said in these verses which cannot be said of King Saul of Israel, of Judas Iscariot, of those crying 'Lord, Lord' in Matthew 7:21-23, of the removed and burned branches of John 15:1-8, and of the ultimately unchanged people mentioned in 2 Peter 2:20-22. If we think that the language of verses 4-5 is too strong to use of unregenerate people, it is because we have not understood an important strand of biblical teaching. We have not grasped how far someone may go, and yet still turn out to be a counterfeit believer. We have not yet got hold of the solemn fact that not every experience of the Holy Spirit is a saving experience.

(iii.) *We must not leave a passage like this without some words of comfort*

At this time I need to speak directly and pastorally to every reader. If you fear that you have committed the blasphemy against the Holy Spirit, and if that fear is constantly propelling you in the direction of our Lord Jesus Christ, it is because you have *not* committed that sin! The passage is intended to terrify us, so that we will fully realise that it is never safe to sin, and that to constantly choose the path of sin is to be lost. But if a fear of apostasy grips your heart and causes you to humble yourself before God, moving you afresh to confess your sin to him and to seek mercy and grace from your High Priest, you have proof enough that you are not an apostate. Apostates do not want to repent; nor can they.

Falling away is a deliberate act, as we have seen. It is calling light darkness. It is treating Jesus as nothing, and consequently shaming him openly. By all means be terrified of doing this, but see that the warning we have studied is, in fact, a gift of God's kindness. By heeding it, you will remain on the path of eternal life. The professing Christian who fails and fails, but who constantly keeps returning to the Lord, has nothing to fear. It is sinners who are instructed to come *boldly* to the throne of grace (4:16). Your High Priest is sympathetic, tender, inviting, forgiving and strengthening; no returning sinner has anything different to say about him. We are safe at his feet. The warning is telling us that we are not safe anywhere else.

10

ENCOURAGEMENT!

PLEASE READ HEBREWS 6:9-20

With the strong exhortation and warning of Hebrews 6:1-8 still ringing in our ears, we now come to something completely different. The rest of the chapter is filled with encouragement and promises.

When someone gives us a stern warning, we are often tempted to think that they do not like us very much; we may even think that they are against us. The apostle is obviously aware of this, and so immediately calls his readers 'beloved' (verse 9). The person who has warned them so bluntly has, in fact, a heart burning with love.

Endless warnings often reduce people to blank despair. Warnings are necessary, but all of us need encouragement as well. The apostle now gives lots of it, and he does so in two ways: first of all he tells the Hebrews two things, and then he underlines what he has said by means of two illustrations.

1. Two things to say

(i.) 'We are confident...' (6:9-10)

6:9: 'Although I have been talking to you about the awful things which happen to apostates and have been giving you a genuine warning, I am convinced in my own mind that you are not such people. As far as you are concerned, I am confident of better things. Speaking personally, I am sure that you are not among those who are going to be lost, but that you are saved people.'

That is an amazing thing to say! If they go back they will prove him wrong, and he has faithfully warned them about where that will lead. But he is sure in his own mind that they are genuine believers. What makes him so sure? It is important to answer this question, for it will show to us how any of us can be sure of our salvation.

Is it because the Hebrews have had a new and marvellous experience of God? Does he base his conviction on that? Not at all . . .

> 6:10: 'It is by looking at your lives that I have come to this conclusion. You are people who have been serving each other, and that is something you continue to do. You do not do it just when the fancy takes you; it is a work and labour that you give yourself to. And what is your motive? It is love; and also concern for God's name.
>
> 'As I look at you, I see your changed lives. I see the fruit of the Spirit there. Self-sacrificing love, the chief fruit and one of the distinctive traits of true Christians, is certainly something everyone can see in you. God is righteous and he will not overlook this fact; you *must* be Christians.'

The Hebrews were spiritually immature and, even worse, they were thinking of renouncing the Christian faith. This was enough for the apostle to issue them real warning. On the other hand, their lives had been sufficiently changed for the apostle to conclude that he was writing to genuine believers. It is a changed life that makes a person's profession of faith credible. Nothing else will do.

This said, there is still sufficient concern in his heart for the apostle to say a second thing to them . . .

(ii.) *We desire . . .* '(6:11-12)

> 6:11: 'You are making a great effort to serve each other, but I want each one of you to make the same effort to go forward spiritually, and to do so to the end, without ever letting up. I want you to keep making spiritual progress until you come to the point where all

doubts are removed (both in your mind and mine) and you are fully sure and certain that your hope is not an empty hope, but securely founded.'

All of us who are pastors have a similar concern for our people. Frankly, we are not at all sure that all our church members are true believers, and many of them are not sure themselves. There are others, however, who have such clarity of belief, and such loving and holy lives, that we nurse no doubts about them at all. Of course, we are fallible. We are well aware that only the Lord knows who truly belongs to him (*2 Tim.* 2:19), and that we are going to have many shocks, both in this life and the next. This does not alter our desire to see our people make such constant and obvious progress in the things of God, that we nurse no serious doubts about any of them.

> 6:12: 'I long to see you shaking off the laziness which, at the moment, characterises your Christian lives. As far as spiritual progress is concerned, you never seem to put yourself out, or to inconvenience yourself in any way. If your faith was obvious (11:1), if your stickability was beyond question, if the characteristic of perseverance which marked out the men and women of faith of former times was clearly seen in you, then I could be as certain of you inheriting the promises made to *you* as of them inheriting the promises made to *them.*'

The apostle, then, has two things to say, and they can be summarised like this:

> 'I have warned you that if you go back, you will be lost. As it happens, I am persuaded in my own mind that you are genuine believers. This is because of your changed lives. But, oh, if only I could have every doubt removed! This would happen if you were more like the godly men and women that we read about in biblical history.'

That is the point of this whole passage and, in many respects, of the whole epistle. The apostle now underlines and enforces what he has just said by means of two illustrations.

2. *Two illustrations*

(i.) *One from Scripture: Abraham* (6:13-18)

6:13: 'Think about Abraham for a moment. God gave him a marvellous promise and reinforced it with an oath made in the greatest name possible—his own!'

6:14-15: 'And what was that promise? It is recorded in Genesis 22:17. It was that Abraham would be blessed and that his descendants would be multiplied. Humanly speaking, it seemed impossible that this promise could be fulfilled, because his wife Sarah was barren and his first son Ishmael had been rejected by God. Nonetheless, Abraham believed the promise and kept on believing it. His confidence had its ups and downs, but he remained God's man, fully trusting him and never walking out on him.

'At last Isaac was born, but that was not the end of Abraham's trials. God told him to offer him up as a sacrifice. However, Abraham kept on trusting, following, worshipping, loving, and obeying God. At the last moment, Isaac was spared and, figuratively speaking, Abraham received him back from the dead. To Isaac were born Esau and Jacob, by which time the promise was well on the way to fulfillment, not only physically, but spiritually, because Abraham is not just the physical father of the Jews but the spiritual father of all believers.

'What characterised that man of God? It was the fact that he went on and on believing. He patiently endured, because that is the way that a person obtains what God has promised. Oh, how I wish the same characteristic was equally obvious in your lives!'

6:16-18: 'Abraham persevered because the promise was reliable. God underlined its certainty by means of an oath, knowing that among men an oath puts a pledge beyond all dispute. In this way, God put his own authority and integrity on the line, to stress that he really meant what he was saying.

'When a promise is that sure, you can patiently endure, knowing that *come what may* it will be fulfilled. And so it was that Abraham persevered in believing. What we need to realise is that the promises made to us are no less sure. God cannot lie. What he says comes to us both as a promise and an oath. This should be a great comfort to us. There is no doubt that God means what he says: those who flee to the Saviour for refuge have a hope that is certain and sure.

'What this means is that if we fail to get to heaven, if we fail to enter into what God has promised, it will not be because the promise has failed. It will not be because God has let us down. It will be because we have failed to continue holding on to what he promised. We have let go. We have not—*come what may*—patiently stuck to believing what God has said. It will be because we have walked out and not demonstrated the perseverance and stickability that Abraham displayed in identical circumstances, a perseverance that led him to obtain what was promised.'

That is the end of the apostle's illustration taken from Scripture. But he does not change subject. Writing of the hope that we have, and how we may be certain of entering into it, he now switches to an illustration taken from the daily life of first-century Mediterranean people.

(ii.) *One from daily life: a ship entering harbour* (6:19-20)

Like everyone else living in the countries surrounding the Mediterranean Sea, every one of the original readers would have been aware of the practice to which the apostle now refers. In every harbour there was a great stone—some examples of which can still be seen today. In some harbours there were many of them. Each such stone was securely and immovably embedded by the water's edge and was known in Latin as an *anchoria,* and in Greek as an *agkura*. Small vessels were moored to it; but it had another purpose.

The science of sailing was not as far advanced as it is today; for example, the rudder had not yet been invented. Very often, by means of its sails alone, a ship could not get into harbour, especially if the wind was against it. When this happened, one of the crew would go ahead in a rowing boat. This man, who was known as 'the forerunner', would attach a line from the struggling ship to the *anchoria*, which was 'sure and steadfast'. Those remaining on the ship simply had to hold on to the line and, by patient and persevering effort, to pull on it. If they did this, without letting go or slackening their effort, they arrived safely in port *every time!*

If we now read verses 19-20 they will come alive in a new way. All of us who are believers nurse the hope that the gospel proclaims. That hope is an *anchoria*, an *agkura*, 'sure and steadfast' and 'behind the veil'—that is, in heaven itself. The forerunner has safely arrived there and attached the line. All we now have to do is to hold on to the hope and never to let go. If we endure, making a patient and persistent effort to do this, every one of us will arrive in harbour, whatever storms, doubts, or difficulties we are currently facing.

There is no need for us to be swamped by any of the waves that contrary winds bring our way. Nor do we need something 'special' to happen to us. If any of us are now lost, it will not be because the forerunner has not done his work; it will not be because the *anchoria* is insecure; it will only be because we loosened our grip and stopped holding on. It will be because we stopped exposing ourselves to the Word of God and no longer availed ourselves of the ministry of our great High Priest.

This high priest is a 'high priest for ever according to the order of Melchizedek'. We shall discover next what exactly that means.

11

A HIGH PRIEST FOR EVER ACCORDING TO THE ORDER OF MELCHIZEDEK

PLEASE READ HEBREWS 7:1-28

In previous chapters the apostle has made it plain that if we are going to make progress in the Christian life, we must understand what it means for the Lord Jesus Christ to be our high priest. He has told us that he is merciful, faithful, and approachable. But he has also said something mysterious: three times he has told us that Christ is a 'high priest for ever after the order of Melchizedek'. What exactly does that mean? Chapter 7, to which we now come, tells us.

The original readers of Hebrews, as we know, were Jews. They had become Christians, but were now seriously considering renouncing their Christianity and returning to the Judaism they had left. For 1,500 years they and their ancestors had looked to the descendants of Aaron to be their priests—to represent them before God and to offer sacrifices for sins and various gifts on their behalf. On becoming Christians they had been told to turn from this Aaronic priesthood (which they knew had been set up by God) and to accept Jesus as their high priest. They were to do this even though he did not come from the priestly tribe of Levi, but from the kingly tribe of Judah (verse 14).

If he was going to stop them going back to Judaism, the apostle needed to convince them that the one he told them to accept as their high priest possessed a priesthood superior to the Aaronic priesthood. He also had to prove that Jesus had been appointed by God to replace the priests of that order. It is this that he now proves conclusively as he fully explains what it means for Christ to be a 'high priest for ever after the order of Melchizedek'.

This chapter is a single unit and we will study it as such. This means that we will not be able to pause over every word and phrase. It seems to me that it is far more important to grasp the central thrust of the apostle's teaching than to risk getting confused by considering too much detail. The essential thing is that we should see that the apostle is here stating five important truths, and that we should be crystal clear as to what each one is.[1]

1. Christ's priesthood is of a higher order than that of the priests of Judaism (7:1-10)

There are two great priests in the Old Testament—Melchizedek and Aaron. Of the two, Melchizedek is the greater. Christ is greater than the priests the Jews were used to because, as Psalm 110:4 declares, he is a high priest, not after the order of Levi (as the Aaronic priests were) but of Melchizedek.

Genesis 14:18-24 tells us about this Melchizedek, and it would be a good idea if we stopped at this point, and read that passage carefully.

The passage records a historical incident which occurred while Abraham was returning home with his spoils of war after a successful military campaign. Melchizedek, who was king of Salem (later known as Jerusalem), but who was also the priest of the Most High God, met him. Melchizedek brought out bread and wine for Abraham and his troops, blessed him in God's name, and told him that he owed his military victory to God. In response, Abraham gave him one-tenth of all that he and his men were carrying.

Where was Levi when all this happened? He was one day to be a descendant of Abraham, but this incident took place long before he was born. In the words of verse 10, 'he was still in the loins of his father when Melchizedek met him.' This fact is significant. Melchizedek is obviously greater than Abraham, because he blessed Abraham; he must, then, be greater than Levi, who was in Abraham's loins at the time. Melchizedek is obviously greater than Abraham, because Abraham paid him tithes (verse 4, 6-7). He would not have done this if Melchizedek had not been entitled to them. We can say, then, that Levi also paid Melchizedek tithes, because he was in Abraham's loins at the time. Yes, Levi, who with his descendants had a right to Israel's tithes (verse 5), actually paid tithes to Melchizedek! (verses 9-10).

Now Psalm 110:4 announces that the Lord Jesus Christ is a high priest 'for ever', not after the order of the lesser (Levi) but of the greater (Melchizedek). This Melchizedek was both a king and a priest (verse 1). So is Jesus; but Levi never was. Melchizedek was 'king of righteousness' (because, translated, that is exactly what his name means) and also 'king of peace' (because 'Salem' means peace). In that way he was a 'type', or Old Testament prefigurement, of the Christ who was to come (verses 2-3).

There are also other ways in which he prefigures the coming Christ. For example, he appears on the stage of history seeming to have no genealogy; at least, none is recorded (verse 3). There is no record that he owes his priesthood to anybody else. Nor is there any record of his death (verses 3, 8). In all these ways he is a picture of the one who 'remains a priest continually'. The reality is Christ (verse 3); Melchizedek is simply a portrait of the Son of God who does not inherit his priesthood (because he has it by right) and who has no successor in it (because it is his eternally).

This is the thrust of what the apostle says in verses 1-10, and it is from there that he moves on to state a second important truth:

2. Christ's priesthood is more effective than that of the priests of Judaism (7:11-19)

The Levitical priesthood and all the ceremonial law connected with it could never bring anything to perfection; but Christ, in *his* high-priestly ministry can, and does (verse 19). This is the point that the apostle now establishes.

The basic argument of this section is easy to follow. Psalm 110:4 emphatically predicted that the Messiah, when he came, would not be a Levitical priest. He would belong to a different order (verse 17), would come from a different tribe (verses 13-14), and would not exercise his priesthood by virtue of a commandment relating to fleshly considerations, but by the authority and power of having an endless life (verse 16). If the Levitical priesthood could have done for the sinner everything that *needed* doing, there would have been no need for another order of priesthood (verse 11). The simple fact that the Messiah was to belong to a different order of priesthood was proof enough that the Levitical order did not, and never could, meet the sinner's needs.

However, if the Levitical priesthood was to be set aside for another order of priesthood, it follows that all the rites, ceremonies, and sacrifices that went with that priesthood were to be set aside too. This is obvious, because the whole system of law revolved round, and was intimately connected with, that priesthood (verses 11-12). It was the lynchpin that held everything together. The end of the Levitical priesthood would spell the end of the whole spectrum of Jewish law.

As was explained earlier (and will be explained again later) that whole system was temporary and imperfect. It consisted of 'types', that is, of pictorial prefigurements of spiritual realities, not of the realities itself. It was therefore weak, of no permanent value, and totally unable to bring anything to perfection. The point of the

Levitical system was not to be an end in itself, but to keep alive a better hope and to bring it in. When that happened, and we were enabled to 'draw near to God' in reality, and not just in picture, there was no longer any need for it. It was therefore set aside (verses 18-19). Its great moral principles remain perpetually valid, because they are rooted in God's nature and character, and are therefore unchangeable. This, however, is not the apostle's subject here. His point is that in God's plan the Levitical system disappeared when Christ came and completed his work.

3. Christ's priesthood is more firmly established than that of the priests of Judaism (7:20-22)

How did an Old Testament priest enter into his office? He had to be born into the tribe of Levi and into the correct family. He simply grew up, and when he became thirty he entered automatically into his priestly work. Nothing else was required, not even an oath of allegiance. It was as straightforward as that.

How did Jesus enter into his priesthood? Verses 20-22 give us the answer. He was established in his office by an oath, not given by himself, but by God. God made it clear that his oath was irreversible, as he said to his Son, 'You are a priest for ever after the order of Melchizedek.' In this way Jesus became a surety and guarantee of a better covenant. It is as clear as can be that his priesthood is more firmly established than that of the priests of Judaism.

4. Christ's priesthood is of longer duration than that of the priests of Judaism (7:23-25)

No Old Testament priest lived for ever. One generation of priests gave way to another. It was thus a priesthood marked by constant change. New priests were constantly coming in on their thirtieth birthday while older ones were retiring or dying. The priesthood remained, but there was no particular priest you could rely on all the time.

With the Lord Jesus Christ, things are not like that at all. His priesthood was given to him personally and is not hereditary. It cannot be passed on to somebody else, nor does it need to be, because 'he continues for ever' (verse 24). He lives for ever and never dies. This means that when we come to God by him, he is always there, always available and never absent. Being all-powerful, there is nobody he cannot help. Whatever we have done and however often we come, he never lets us down. His presence in heaven as the sinner's representative guarantees that no one relying on him will ever be turned away. His intercession for the weak and failing sinner is always successful. Verse 25 must surely rank as one of the most wonderful promises of the entire Bible!

5. Christ's priesthood is exactly suited to the sinner's need (7:26–28)

As a sinner, I need a high priest who is not only of superior rank and power, but who is also holy. A high priest who has to offer up sacrifices for his own sins is of no use to me. Such a high priest can certainly be a picture of a better high priest to come, but in and of himself, he cannot help me. I need a high priest who has the right to go into the presence of God to represent me there; a high priest who can go only into a *picture* of heaven is not really the high priest that I need.

Only a high priest who is himself holy can have the right to go into God's immediate presence and to bear up my cause there. He must be a man, because I am a man. I need him to speak for me, but not to have to speak for himself first. I need a high priest whose intercession for me is certain to prevail. The Lord Jesus Christ is such a high priest. He is exactly what I need.

Jesus is not a Levitical priest, living with sin, infirmity, and weakness, and every day offering up sacrifices for himself as well as for others. Appointed to his task by a divine oath, and fully qualified for his work, he has been appointed to it for ever! He has dealt with sin decisively, once for all, by offering himself up as a perfect sacrifice, fully acceptable to God, in whose very presence he now stands.

What a wonderful passage this is! God is holy, but I am a sinner. Is there anybody who can approach God on my behalf—someone who is unstained by sin, elevated to the highest heaven, and appointed by God to an eternal, unchanging, and availing priesthood? This passage is telling me that there is!

With Jesus Christ as my high priest, there will never be an occasion when I approach God but find that I have been turned away. Because of his intercession, there will never be a day when I will find that I am condemned to live out of fellowship with God. His intercession for sinners is perfect and successful. I can always come to him with confidence, knowing that I will be certain to obtain both mercy for my sins and grace to help in my need. And all this is true because he exercises a priesthood that is in every way superior to the shadowy priesthood of Old Testament days.

If this were not true, I would have to live and die without hope. But it is true! So why would anyone want to turn away from him? Backsliding is foolishness; apostasy is madness.

12

THE MEDIATOR OF
A BETTER COVENANT

PLEASE READ HEBREWS 8:1-13

The writer to the Hebrews is a brilliant teacher. Having brought his hearers up a steep slope of learning, he now gives them a moment to catch their breath. He begins this chapter by summarising and developing what he has said so far, before proceeding to gently lead them on to even higher ground.

1. A summary (8:1-5)

8:1-2: 'The real point I have been making so far is this—we Christian believers have a high priest who is unique. He is superior to the prophets, to the angels, to Moses, to Joshua and to Aaron. He is an eternal priest after the order of Melchizedek who can do for the sinner all that the sinner *needs* doing. He is able to save men and women now, totally and for ever.

'*This* is the high priest we have, and he is on a throne. He exercises his ministry in heaven where he occupies a royal position. Although he is but one person, he exercises two offices—that of a priest and that of a king. He does not minister in the tabernacle or temple, that is, in the earthly shadow of a heavenly reality. No, he ministers in the heavenly reality itself. He does not exercise his priesthood in an earthly tent pitched by men. That tent is only a pictorial representation of the real thing, and it is there that he ministers—in the dwelling place of God himself!'

8:3: 'Now the whole essence of priesthood lies in this: a man appears before God on behalf of other people, and presents gifts and sacrifices. If Christ is *really* a high priest, that is what he must be doing—and he is!'

It is interesting to note that the apostle does not tell us at this point *what* Christ is offering. He will tell us this in 9:13-14. We will see there that he is in heaven as one who has finished his work of offering, and that he sits there as one who has completed his work. His presence in heaven speaks to us of the fact that his offering was once for all. It is over. It cannot possibly be repeated and never will be.

8:4: 'Christ's priesthood is not exercised here on earth. As I write to you, there are still plenty of priests doing that. I am speaking of the superior high priest who is glorified above, and whose priesthood is associated with heaven and not earth. If I was talking about an earthly priesthood, Christ would not be doing it, the reason being that those priests have to belong to the family of Aaron, with which family Christ has nothing to do.'

8:5: 'Those priests do not exercise a real priestly ministry. They are only imperfect, shadowy, pictorial representations of heavenly realities. The real dwelling-place of God is not an earthly tent but heaven. God instructed Moses to make a sanctuary that was an earthly copy and shadow of what is in heaven. He did this to convey to our poor minds some idea of invisible and spiritual realities. Our Lord's ministry is not exercised in that physical representation, but in heaven itself. *This* is the high priest that we have!'

'We have such a high priest'! The whole purpose of the first seven chapters of Hebrews has been to get across to us the surpassing greatness of Christ, and in *that* context to show us why apostasy is a peril. If you walk out on the glory of God, there is nowhere to go except into outer darkness.

Each one of us needs to ask ourselves whether we have truly grasped this point—there is no one greater than our Lord Jesus Christ! Seated in heaven at this moment is someone who is God, who has come among us as a man, and who, as the God-Man, is superior to all the prophets, to all the angels, and to the godliest of men. He represents his people in heaven itself and ensures their perfect acceptance there.

If we have grasped this point, we are now ready for the next one, which the apostle teaches in the remainder of this chapter and throughout chapter 9. It can be summarised in the words of verse 6: 'But now he has obtained a more excellent ministry . . .'

The emphasis up until now has been on the superiority of the *person* of our high priest. That emphasis is now going to shift. From now on it will be on the superiority of his *ministry*. There is no one greater than Christ. We have seen that this is true as we have considered who he is; we shall now see that it is equally true when we consider what he has done.

'He has obtained a more excellent ministry.' His ministry is as much superior as he himself is superior. This is clear for three reasons. He is 'mediator of a better covenant'; we shall learn about this next, in 8:6-13. In addition, he is the priest of a better tabernacle, and the offerer of a better sacrifice; these two reasons will be covered in chapter 9. To teach these truths the apostle will no longer return to Christ's being a high priest for ever after the order of Melchizedek. Instead, he will once more contrast Christ's work with that of the Levitical priesthood, to which the original readers were particularly attracted.

2. Christ is mediator of a better covenant (8:6-13)

This fact is stated in 8:6 and expounded in 8:6-13. We will understand it easily enough if we ask and answer four questions:

(i.) *What is a covenant?*

A covenant is a binding agreement, or contract, between two or more parties. The norm is two. In a covenant one party promises to do certain things on condition that the other party does certain things. For example, when a house is sold, one party agrees to give up his ownership of the property and to hand it over to the other, on condition that the second party pays a certain sum of money.

That is the way it is with men and women. With God, however, it is different, as the Bible clearly reveals. A covenant involving God is more of a one-sided agreement where he, as the superior party, promises extraordinary benefits, but also dictates terms which are not open to negotiation.

To see this, we need only to think of God's covenant with Israel at Mount Sinai. Having chosen the Israelites, redeemed them and conquered them, he promises them blessings and dictates terms. He will be their God and will take them to be his people. On their side, they must be fully obedient to everything that he requires of them, whether it be in matters of right or wrong, or in matters of worship or national government. This is true of what he commands them at Sinai, what he has previously commanded, or what he is yet to command. If they obey, they will enjoy the promised blessings; but if they do not obey, they will forfeit the blessings and, instead, experience God's curses.

Verse 6 is saying that by means of Christ, and into our hands, has come a better covenant than that. It is better because it is founded on better promises.

(ii.) *Why was a new covenant needed?* (8:7-8a)

If the old covenant had worked, there would never have been any need to replace it. The fact is, however, that it did not meet the sinner's need. It brought nobody into an intimate walk with God. It brought nobody to enjoy him.

It lacked power, and yet the fault did not lie as much with the covenant as with the people (verse 8a). They did not live in full obedience to the Lord. The outcome was that God eventually rejected the Jewish nation as his special people, as our Lord explained in so many of his parables. If men and women were ever therefore to know God as their God, and to have the privilege and enjoyment of being his people, there would have to be a different covenant. The covenant of Sinai brought nobody to that position. Something else was needed.

(iii.) *Was such a covenant ever promised?* (8:8-9, 13)

It certainly was—repeatedly. Take what Jeremiah said in his book (31:31-34) and here quoted in verses 8-9. At that time the prophet was in despair; he saw no hope of the apostate nation ever walking with God. The Lord revealed to him that he would make a new covenant which would stand in marked contrast to the one that they had failed to keep, and which had brought them into judgement. By means of this new covenant God's law would be in their hearts, and not just in a written code; they would at last enjoy the covenant blessings they had never entered into; they would have a personal and intimate knowledge of God; and all their sins would be forgiven and never again called to mind.

This was not the only indication in Old Testament days that another covenant was on the way, but what was striking about God's words to Jeremiah was his use of the word 'new' (verses 8, 13). You cannot have a 'new covenant' without making the existing one old. And once a thing is 'old' you know that it is nearing the end of its days; it is on the way out and will soon be replaced; it is obsolete; it is ready to disappear.

The Hebrews should have understood that their sacred Scriptures had made it clear that a new covenant was on the way. God had announced that what they so greatly revered was going to be replaced. It is this new covenant which has been mediated to sinners by our Lord Jesus Christ.

(iv.) *There has been mention of 'better promises', so what are they?* (8:10-12)

Many of the promises of the Old Covenant were concerned with this present life. They covered such subjects as personal prosperity, length of life, and national privileges. But the promises of the new covenant (as we shall see) are totally concerned with spiritual blessings, both now and in the life to come.

In the Old Covenant, God said, in effect, 'If you will . . . I will.' The covenant blessings were conditioned upon human obedience. In the new covenant God says, 'I will . . .' It is interesting to see how many times this occurs in verses 7-12. Although it is not plain from these verses, except by implication, the fact is that these blessings are conditioned upon *Christ's* obedience. *He* is the mediator of the New Covenant.

Let us take a moment to notice again the specific promises which the new covenant makes. It promises that God will put his law in our mind and write them on our hearts (verse 10). But what does that mean? The Jews of the Old Testament had no real inclination to obey God's commandments, as their history repeatedly proved. They had the outward code, but their hearts were not in love with it. The New Covenant believer is entirely different. He can say, 'I delight in the law of God according to the inward man' (*Rom.* 7:22). God's law is not just a text book to him; it is something which he loves in his heart of hearts. Deep down inside him he has a desire to please the Lord and to walk in his ways. This inner transformation is one of the blessings of the New Covenant.

Another promise from God is also voiced in verse 10: 'I will be their God, and they shall be my people.' The Israelites of old knew that they were God's chosen people and were very quick to remind surrounding nations that they did not enjoy the same privilege. The fact is, however, that the individual Israelite of Old Testament days was not very bothered about walking with God and pleasing him, and enjoyed no intimate relationship with him. The New Testament believer, however, has the Holy Spirit in his heart, by which he cries out to God, 'Abba, Father' (*Rom.* 8:15-17). He knows himself to be God's child and feels bound to him by the bonds of family affection.

Linked to this is what is mentioned in verse 11. The Levites taught the Word of God to ancient Israel, but that Word remained largely on the surface. But under the New Covenant every believer—even those who are boys and girls—knows the Lord. Knowing God personally is one of the promised blessings.

A further promise is found in verse 12. Although Old Testament people constantly offered sacrifices such as bulls, lambs, or pigeons, they never enjoyed any flooding sense of forgiveness, pardon, and peace with God. All their ritual was only a shadowy picture of the better covenant to come. Those of us who have come to the Lord Jesus Christ are considered perfect before God; this is because our sins have been put to Christ's account on the cross, and his righteousness has been reckoned to our account. His sacrifice has dealt with our sins, not in picture, but in reality. We now enjoy pardon for our sins—the sins of our nature, open sins, secret sins, repeated sins, yesterday's sins, today's sins, tomorrow's sins, whether these be actual transgressions or sins of omission—every sin! God does not remember any of them any more.

Putting all this together, we can say that the New Covenant promises us a changed and obedient heart, the privilege of belonging to the Lord, intimacy with him, and total and perpetual pardon. No wonder the apostle says of Christ that he is 'the mediator of a better covenant, which was established on better promises'! (verse 6).

Does any reader long for the blessings that we have just described? No religion, not even Old Testament religion, can give them to you. They are Jesus Christ's gift to everyone who comes to him. So do not stay away. Come to him—now!

Are you a believer who is yearning for more blessing in your life? You will not find it by seeking after some mystical experience. All God's blessings are in Jesus Christ's hands; he is the mediator of the New Covenant. Come to him afresh. Confess your need to him. Close in on him. Only by renewing your communion with him will you ever experience the spiritual refreshing you want so much.

As you read through this book, are you rejoicing in Christ? Face this, then: your contentment and joy are not due to any merit of your own. Every blessing which a sinner ever enjoys comes to him through the Lord Jesus Christ. It is a gift of his grace.

It is time for all of us to thank him again for all that he has done. He has done what he has done because he is who he is. Consider him. Fill your mind with thoughts about him. Look away from yourself and fix your eyes on 'the author and finisher of our faith' (12:2). The person who does this need never fear apostasy, because his heart will cry out something like this:

> Since mine eyes were fixed on Jesus,
> I've lost sight of all beside;
> So enchained my spirit's vision,
> Looking at the Crucified.[1]

'Lord, to whom shall we go? You have the words of eternal life' (*John* 6:68).

13

THE PRIEST OF
A BETTER TABERNACLE

PLEASE READ HEBREWS 9:1-14

We have seen how the apostle looked at the Old Covenant, and then at the New Covenant which our Lord Jesus Christ has brought in, and how he has concluded that Christ is the 'mediator of a better covenant'.

With that in mind, he now looks at the tabernacle in which the Old Testament Levitical priests ministered. That tabernacle, although beautiful and impressive, still did not give the sinner real access to God. However, this is something which Christ, who ministers in heaven itself, *has* brought about. He is the priest of a better tabernacle.

How does the apostle teach us this truth? His approach is very simple and easy to follow. First of all he looks at the old tabernacle and at six objects that were found there, and concludes that the old dispensation gave no real access into God's presence (verses 1-10). Then, by way of contrast, he looks at what Christ has done and at where he now ministers. In doing so, he lists seven facts, and concludes by assuring us that through him we have *real* access (verses 11-14). If we keep this outline in mind, we shall have no trouble at all understanding this section.

1. How it was: six objects—no access! (9:1-10)

9:1: 'Let us go back to Old Testament days and remember what things were like then. God had given all sorts of instructions about how he was to be worshipped, as you well know. That worship took place in a tabernacle, that is, a tent-sanctuary, which was located here on earth.'

9:2: 'Yes, God's sanctuary was a tent! It was divided into two distinct parts, each part having its own furniture. The first part, called 'the sanctuary' or "the holy place", contained the lampstand to give light, a table on which to put the special shewbread, and, of course, the shewbread itself.'

9:3: 'What went on in that first part was hidden from public view, the tabernacle wall acting, if you like, as a sort of veil. The public could go into the tabernacle courtyard, but only the priests could enter here. However, separating this first room from the second, known as "the Holiest of all" or "the Holy of Holies", was an enormous curtain, which we can call 'the second veil'. The two rooms were thus divided from each other.'

9:4: 'The Holy of Holies contained the golden altar of incense.'

We must not hastily conclude that the apostle is making a mistake in saying this, as many writers seem to think. The fact is that the ministry of that altar was more linked and connected to the Holy of Holies than it was to the Holy Place, but, for reasons of access, it had to be on the accessible side of the veil, and not behind it.

9:4-5: 'Also in the Holy of Holies was the ark of the covenant. On the outside, this was overlaid on all sides with gold. Inside it were the golden pot containing a sample of the manna, Aaron's rod that budded, and the two tablets of stone on which were written the terms of the covenant—the Ten Commandments. Above it were the cherubim of glory overshadowing the mercy seat. Of all these things we cannot now speak in detail.'

There is no doubt, of course, that each of these objects was a 'type', that is, a symbolic prefigurement of the coming Christ. The apostle does not explain all that here, because his purpose is not to give a detailed exposition of everything that the tabernacle signified but, rather, to contrast the ministry of that tabernacle with what the Lord Jesus Christ has done, and is still doing.

9:6: 'This is what God ordained, and when all was ready the Old Testament priests went in and out of the first room, doing their work—tending the lamp, changing the shewbread, and obtaining ceremonial cleansing for the people at the altar of incense.'

9:7: 'But that is as far as it went, and no further. Those priests *never* went into the Holy of Holies. The only person who *ever* went there was the high priest. When he did this he went alone, and only once a year. Even then he never went in by right, but carrying the blood of a sacrifice which had been offered for the ignorant sins of the people whom he represented, but also for himself—because he too was a sinner needing atonement.'

9:8: 'Through all this the Holy Spirit was teaching the world a lesson. After all, it was he who had given to Moses the detailed design of the Tabernacle. It was plain that as long as the tabernacle was standing, the way to *really* get into the presence of God had not been openly revealed.'

We can see, then, that the whole purpose of the tabernacle was to be a pictorial representation of spiritual realities. It existed in order to teach great spiritual principles, and thus to prepare people for the coming of Christ. As we look back at it now, it helps us in our understanding of what Christ has done. The fact remains, however, that the Tabernacle's ritual and ceremonies never actually offered any real access into God's presence.

9:9-10: 'Yes, the whole thing was a picture. It offered outward ceremonial cleansing, but never gave to anyone a clear conscience. It was spiritually inadequate; it never did anything for the worshipper as far as his real standing with God was concerned. The whole system spoke of spiritual realities but did not bring the worshipper to experience them. It pointed beyond itself to different days to come and, in doing so, made it clear that it itself was only temporary. The spiritual realities of which it spoke were to be fully revealed at a later period.'

Everything in the tabernacle spoke of the need of cleansing, but it never gave it. It spoke all the time of the need and way of access, but never gave that access. Everything connected with the tabernacle would have been worthless and pointless, if it had not all spoken of something to come! In the Bible the number six is the number of failure. 'Six objects—no access' is an accurate summary of the apostle's teaching given so far in this chapter.

2. How it is: seven facts—access! (9:11-4)

At this point the apostle comes to spell out the contrast between that old ministry and Christ's. How could the Hebrews think of going back to a material, local, and ineffectual ministry while knowing that the ministry of the Lord Jesus Christ is spiritual, non-material, in heaven itself, eternal and availing? He brings out this lesson by unveiling seven facts:[1]

(i.) A better priest (9:11)

The old dispensation constantly pointed beyond itself to better things to come—and those better things have been brought about by the Lord Jesus Christ. The old dispensation spoke of cleansing, not because it was giving it, but because its ceremonies were designed to prepare minds for the cleansing given by Christ. It kept faith alive during the years that people were waiting for him.

It provided us with illustrations which would help us to grasp the significance of what he has now done and the access he has provided. Jesus has brought in what the Old Testament promised, and so is a better priest. At last, a better system has been inaugurated. The Messiah has come!

(ii.) *A better sanctuary* (9:11)

Jesus does not minister in a localised earthly sanctuary, but in 'the greater and more perfect tabernacle not made with hands, that is, not of this creation'. He ministers in the spiritual reality of which the old Tabernacle was but a picture, that is, in heaven itself.

(iii.) *A better sacrifice* (9:12)

The redemption promised in former times is now a reality. Christ has brought it in, not by shedding the blood of animals or of others, but by shedding his own. He offered up his own life. He himself suffered death. Not only so, but he has entered into the heavenly tabernacle and presented his own blood on the mercy seat there as an atonement.

(iv.) *A better method* (9:12)

Christ has not come with repeated offerings and repeated enterings beyond the veil. No real cleansing or access is provided that way. His offering up of himself took place once. He entered into heaven once. He remains there now. Everything about his ministry is infinitely superior!

(v.) *A better blessing* (9:12)

The Old Testament priests entered into their sanctuary with the blood of others, but Christ entered heaven with his own blood. The Old Testament priests obtained only ceremonial cleansing; this they did once a year, but the following year it needed repeating. Christ obtained for us a permanent blessing, called here 'eternal redemption'. Nothing needed repeating. We were well and truly brought back to God—for ever!

(vi.) *A better guarantee* (9:13-14)

If the blood of animals, and all the ritual associated with it, was capable of removing ceremonial defilement, how much more is Christ's sacrifice of himself capable of removing the *actual* guilt and defilement of sin! Upheld by the eternal Spirit as he did it, this is the work that he accomplished. The sinless one voluntarily offered himself up to God. There was nothing momentary or temporary about his work on the cross. The result of this is that believers are inwardly cleansed, enjoy uncondemning consciences, are free from the slightest attempt to rely on works for their salvation, and are brought into the worship and service of the living God.

(vii.) *A better result* (9:13-14)

Yes, the result of Christ's work is that believers are inwardly cleansed and enjoy consciences that no longer condemn them. The ceremonial cleansings of the Old Testament could bring only outward purity. The flesh was washed. Believers, however, are now free from an inward sense of guilt, and from all attempts to rely on works for their salvation. Inwardly transformed, they are now changed into people who truly worship and serve the living God. They have thus been brought into blessings which Jewish ritual could not even think of offering. Not only do they have real access to the Lord, but they have also been appointed to his service.

That is how it was, and that is how it is. The apostle is telling the Hebrew Christians to look:[2]

• Not to the Jewish priests, but to the Lord Jesus Christ.

• Not to the Tabernacle made with hands, but to the greater and more perfect tabernacle made by God himself—to heaven, his dwelling-place.

•Not to the blood of animals, or to any rites or ceremonies, but to the blood of Christ.

• Not to an annual ceremonial cleansing obtained for Israel by its high priest, but to the eternal redemption which the Lord Jesus Christ has obtained for all who believe.

The Hebrews would not have considered apostatising if they had mastered one vital point: what matters most in this life and the next is *access*—that is, closing in on God, knowing him savingly, and enjoying him. Christianity, and only Christianity, is a religion of access. No other religion on earth can even offer it. Judaism speaks of it, but it cannot be obtained there. The experience of access, and the basis for it, is explained only in the gospel message. It is a privilege which is enjoyed by believers in Christ and by nobody else at all.

What blessings we have in Christ! Churches committed to the gospel are free from rites and ceremonies, because they know that pictorial representations of spiritual realities have been superseded by the realities themselves. Because of Christ's great work for us, the fact is that believers may enjoy access to their heavenly Father in any place, at any time, and in any circumstances.

How poor unbelievers are! Oh, that they would understand that *access* is what the Lord Jesus Christ offers to them! Oh, that they would ask for it and receive it!

How sad it is, however, when believers forget and neglect the wonderful privilege which Christ has given to them. Can there be any better way of expressing our gratitude to him than by availing ourselves of it—by going through life as a man or woman of prayer, by walking with him all the way to heaven, by enjoying our God on the basis of who the Lord Jesus Christ is and what he has done?

14

THE OFFERER OF
A BETTER SACRIFICE

PLEASE READ HEBREWS 9:14-28

The apostle spent the first seven chapters of his book revelling in who the Lord Jesus Christ is. From 8:1, however, he turned from his *person* to his *work*, from who he is to what he has done.

He is *the mediator of a better covenant*, giving to his people changed hearts that desire to do God's will; bringing each one to know him as God, and as their God, and leading them to experience and enjoy entire forgiveness for their sins.

Not only so, but he is *the priest of a better tabernacle*, giving his people what the Old Testament tabernacle foreshadowed, but could never give anyone—namely, free access into the Holiest of all.

In the passage before us the apostle teaches a third truth about the work of Christ. He continues to contrast what people experienced in Old Testament days with what believers enjoy through the Lord Jesus Christ, but his particular aim is to show us that he is *the offerer of a better sacrifice*.

To make this clear, he takes us through three steps. He shows us:

1. What Christ has done in the past: *he has appeared on earth* (9:14-23).

2. What Christ is doing now: *he is appearing in heaven* (9:24-28a).

3. What Christ will do in the future: *he will appear from heaven and come to earth* (9:28b).

If you like, the apostle invites us to take a look *backwards*, a look *upwards*, and a look *forwards*. As we work through this passage, I invite you to do the same.

1. A look backwards: what Christ has done in the past—he has appeared on earth (9:14-23)

9:14: We looked at this verse in our previous study, but let us remind ourselves of what it says: after living a perfect life out of love for his heavenly Father, Christ went voluntarily to the cross where he spilt his blood. In doing this he was sustained and upheld by the eternal Spirit. His purpose was that we might receive the two great blessings of the new covenant. These are a new record and a new heart. He did it so that we might be truly cleansed from our sins, and also be made willing and able to worship and serve God.

9:15: The old covenant certainly talked about eternal life, forgiveness and cleansing, but it could never give these things, because the blood of animals is simply incapable of providing real atonement for sin. And yet, even at that time, there were people who were 'called', and who entered into 'the promise of the eternal inheritance'. How did this happen? They did not receive such a blessing on the basis of animal sacrifices, but on the basis of the infinitely superior sacrifice which those Old Testament sacrifices spoke about—that is, the sacrifice of our Lord Jesus Christ. It is because he offered such a superior sacrifice that he is able to bring people into the benefits of the New Covenant, both retrospectively as well as from Calvary onwards. Yes, there were saved people in Old Testament days, and every one of them was saved by our Lord Jesus Christ through the work of his cross.

9:16-17: To make this clear, the apostle invites us to think about what happens when someone makes a will. Throughout this illustration he uses the word 'testament' as it is used when someone writes their 'last will and testament'.

As long as the will-writer is alive, he can chop and change his will as he likes. The written will lies on the table, but it has no legal force because its author is still alive. As soon as he dies, everything changes. The will comes into force. Its wording is now beyond all change and emendation, and its provisions are unalterable. How does the will become fixed, certain, and secure? It is by the death of the testator. It is his death which brings all its benefits into operation.

This is a very good illustration, because the New Covenant is not so much a contract between two parties as a donation, at least as far as we are concerned. The Lord Jesus Christ, our covenant Head, covenanted with the Father in eternity that he would save us by living for us and dying for us. All that he promised to secure for us becomes ours by his death. It was at that moment that the penalty due to his people fell on him, meaning that no such penalty awaits them. It was by his *death* that believers entered into pardon.

9:18: The New Covenant could not have come into operation without Christ's blood being shed. Those who find this idea surprising should think back to God's inauguration of his covenant with Israel. This happened at Mount Sinai, where the shedding of blood was a prominent feature.

9:19-20: None of the provisions of that covenant came into force until they were ratified, confirmed and made valid by Moses.

How did he do that? Was it by means of a signature, such as when we confirm our covenants in marriage or the purchase of a house? No; he had to sprinkle both the book of covenant terms and the covenant people with blood, as he said, 'This is the blood of the covenant (or testament) which God has commanded you.'

9:21-22: If we think back to the tabernacle, and to all the furniture and utensils that went with it, we find that none of it could be used until its ceremonial defilement had been removed by the sprinkling of blood. In fact, under Old Testament law, we may almost say that every single object and ritual connected with worship had to be cleansed with blood. Until it was, it was unfit for use.

9:23: The apostle closes this first point by reminding us of what he has told us before: the earthly tabernacle, and everything that went with it, was just a pictorial representation of heavenly realities. It was a visual aid intended to convey to our minds certain spiritual truths which we would not otherwise be able to grasp.

This raises a question: could not an Old Testament worshipper have said something like this: 'Doesn't the Shekinah glory of God dwell here in this earthly tabernacle? Surely then, as this physical place is hallowed by his presence, it does not need any cleansing.'

The tabernacle, by definition, could not in any full and complete sense have been the dwelling place of the infinite God. But even if it could have been, it would still have needed cleansing. This is because it was a place where God met sinners. God is holy, and sinners cannot come to him as they are. Atonement must be made for them. Blood must be shed. Cleansing through sacrifice was an essential part of tabernacle worship.

If that was true of the earthly picture, how much more is it true of the heavenly reality! Animal sacrifices were sufficient for revealing principles and teaching spiritual lessons, but the sacrifice necessary for sinners to approach God in the heavenly reality must be *infinitely* better than they were!

The apostle has made his first point and is now ready for the second. The first point is essential for all that follows, and it has been well made. Wills, testaments, and covenants are made certain and secure by death. The death which makes the New Covenant secure is the death of Christ.

Look backwards. Reflect on what the Lord Jesus Christ has done in the past. He has appeared on earth. He has died the death necessary to save sinners. In this way he has fulfilled in reality all that the Old Testament types spoke about in picture form.

The covenant blessings which the apostle has been writing about are secure. Christ's death has secured them! The fact that we who believe are new creatures in Christ, with all our sins forgiven, having God as our Father and enjoying access to him, is because of Golgotha. Such blessings are mine, as are countless more, because of his cross—but only because of his cross.

> Forbid it, Lord, that I should boast
> Save in the death of Christ my God:
> All the vain things that charm me most,
> I sacrifice them to His blood.[1]

2. A look upwards: what Christ is doing now—he is appearing in heaven (9:24-28a)

9:24: To understand what the apostle says next we must think back to what the Old Testament reveals about Israel's annual Day of Atonement (*Lev.* 16). On that day the high priest killed the appropriate sacrifice and then, with its blood, went into the Holy of Holies. He did this once a year, every year. Unlike him, Christ has not entered into a mere picture of the heavenly reality. He does not minister in a tent erected by humans, which is but a figure of spiritual truths. He ministers in heaven itself, where he appears before God's face (as the original Greek says). And this he does on our behalf.

9:25: How different Christ is from that Old Testament priest! During his lifetime that priest entered the Holy of Holies quite often, that is, once a year. Each entering in was a repetition of what happened the year before. Every time he did it he carried blood which was not his own. But Christ, by virtue of an unrepeatable sacrifice in which he shed his own blood, has entered once and for all. He has gone in to stay!

9:26: Christ's sacrifice is a sufficient offering for sinners. It is a perfect atonement for their sins. This is proved by one simple fact—his sacrifice does not need repeating. If that were not the case, he would have needed to keep repeating his sacrifice from the foundation of the world until now.

Christ's sacrifice took place in time. It happened on a definite date. And yet this once for all sacrifice is sufficient and effective for all believers of all times. This means that it even dealt with the sins of those believers who lived before it took place. It is a sacrifice that does not need anything added to it, because it is not deficient in any way at all. Nor does it need repeating. This is proved by the fact that having offered himself once, Christ has entered into heaven to stay.

Christ has appeared once, towards the end of the world's history. Unlike the Old Testament high priest who offered the blood of others, without any pain to himself, Christ has offered himself. The eternal Son of God endured and experienced mortal agony as he died. If, like the Old Testament high priest, he was required to offer a continual oblation, he would have to die again and again and again. This is clearly impossible.

No; the one offering that he *did* make is perfect, and by virtue of it he appears in heaven continually to represent his people there. Sin's penalty has been fully and really paid. It has been put away. God the Father accepts this; the proof of this is that he accepts into heaven for ever the one who atoned for sin by the sacrifice of himself. No further proof is required of the fact that Christ's sacrifice is never to be repeated.

9:27-28a: Yes, just as certainly as men and women die once, and are judged once, equally certainly has Christ been offered once. In that one single transaction he bore the sin of many.

Let us take a moment to reflect on this teaching and to grasp it completely. When the Lord Jesus Christ died, he bore the full penalty due to his people. He put away their sins. The Father has completely accepted this, and so Christ is perpetually in heaven. He represents us to the Father. But he is not pleading. He is not crying. He is not agonisingly imploring that we should be accepted there. We need to be very clear about what is happening there.

Everything that separates us from God has been dealt with. When the substitute died in our place, every sanction that our sins deserve fell on him. The simple fact that Christ is in heaven, and that he remains there, testifies to this.

His very being in heaven proclaims that there is no punishment left for any believer to bear. There is no sacrifice that now needs to be offered, no atonement that needs to be made. There is nothing left to pay. There is no offering that is still required. There is nothing to bring. All that needs doing has been done, and Christ's simple presence in heaven ensures our acceptance there. His *being there* is enough.

Any attempt to re-offer Christ's sacrifice is to suggest that it was insufficient, or that God needs some reminder of Calvary in addition to the presence of his Son. This is what makes the Roman

Catholic Mass an insult to God. It is a blasphemous ceremony and it is a sin to participate in it.

In the same way, to insist that a sinner must perform some penance or other implies that something additional to Christ's sacrifice is necessary to secure the sinner's full acceptance by God; it is to belittle and to degrade the perfection of what God in Christ secured at Calvary. There is no place for any form of penance in any church that claims to be Christian.

In order to approach God, all a sinner needs to do is to rely on the fact that his sins, which rightly deserve God's wrath, have been fully dealt with at Calvary; and that God has accepted what Christ did on the sinner's behalf. He needs to cast himself upon God's love in Christ, and not to put any faith in anything that he might think he can do, or might hope to do. As long as the Lord Jesus Christ is in heaven, no sinner pleading his name can ever be turned away.

How privileged we believers are! What access is ours! How great is the price that secured it! How great is the love which has been poured out on us! How wise the eternal plan of salvation is! How exalted the Man of Sorrows is now! But the apostle will not allow us simply to revel in the wonder of our salvation. He still has one further thing to say.

3. A look forwards: what Christ will do in the future—he will appear from heaven and come to earth (9:28b)

We did not see the Lord when he came to earth the first time, and we do not see him now. But we love him and we are glad that he will come to earth again, that he 'will descend from heaven with a shout' (*1 Thess.* 4:16), and that he will do this without ever leaving heaven! At his coming the present distinctions between visible and invisible, material and spiritual, earthly and heavenly, will be broken down, as the book of Revelation makes clear (*Rev.* 21:1-5). On that momentous day the Lord of heaven, without leaving heaven, will come from heaven and 'appear a second time'.

Meanwhile, we eagerly wait for him and look for him, knowing that we shall not be disappointed. How different his second coming will be from his first! This time he will not come to deal with sin; this he has done, as we have seen. He will not come to save sinners, but to collect all sinners who have been saved by the shedding of his blood.

The day of Christ's return will be the final display of the superiority of the New Covenant over the Old. The New Covenant not only gives us access to God now, but an eternal home in his heavenly glory! That is where our crucified Redeemer is at this moment, and his presence there secures our acceptance. But where he is, we shall be also. For us to get there, he will actually come again to this earth to collect us.

That wonderful day, for which we eagerly wait, will be the climax and final consummation of God's plan of salvation. What a hope we have! Who can tell what joys and glories lie ahead of us? The apostle will not let us forget it. It is something to think about every day. But we must also reflect on the fact that all this too was secured for us by the Saviour's cross and shame.

We are going to heaven! We are going to heaven! Christ is coming to take us there, but no one will get there without him. Those, like the Hebrews, who are thinking of walking out on him, would do well to remember this.

15

UNDERLINING AND ENFORCING

PLEASE READ HEBREWS 10:1-18

The Epistle to the Hebrews is basically about the greatness of Christ. There is nobody like him! He is unique and he is superior. This is true both when we reflect on *who he is,* as chapters 1-7 have shown us, and when we consider *what he has done,* which has been the apostle's theme since 8:1.

This is still the theme in the passage now before us. In this section the apostle does not tell us anything new, which we may find something of a relief. Instead, he spends his time underlining and enforcing what he has been saying since 8:1. He says what he has already said, but in a slightly different way. He does not want the Hebrews, or us, to miss his meaning: what the Lord Jesus Christ has done is infinitely superior to the covenant, priesthood, and sacrifices that the original readers were thinking of going back to.

How, then, does the apostle start this section? What does he underline first?[1]

1. The ineffectiveness of the old sacrifices (10:1-4)

> 10:1a: 'Think again about the Old Testament sacrifices that we have been mentioning. They were shadows. They were earthly represen-
> tations and pictures. They spoke of better things to come, but they
> were *not* those better things.'

10:1b-2: 'Year in, year out, those old sacrifices were repeated. But they never actually *did* anything for the sinner. They never actually dealt with sin. If they had have done something lasting and effectual, they would not have needed repeating.'

To illustrate this, let us assume that you have a nasty cough. I produce a bottle of medicine and say to you, 'Take this. It will cure you.' You take it, but feel no better. So you take it again; and then again. Years later, you are *still* taking it!

What is that medicine doing for you? Nothing! The proof is that you are still coughing, despite the fact that you are taking the medicine. *All* that the medicine is doing is to remind you that your cough really does need a cure!

10:2b-3: 'If Old Testament sacrifices had really dealt with sin, then Old Testament consciences would have been cleansed. This never happened. All that the sacrifices managed to do was to constantly remind people of their sin and of their need of cleansing.'

Under the old regime, worshippers remained unforgiven, except that this very fact awakened faith in some of them. As we have seen earlier in the book, they came to rely on the *coming* sacrifice, and were cleansed from their sins by means of their faith in *that*.

10:4: 'For it is a straightforward fact that the shedding of animal blood cannot deal with the sin which separates you from God and consigns you to hell.'

How could it? Think it out—how could it? How can *anything* like that remove sin? It is an obvious impossibility. Fully realising this will prepare us for the next point.

2. The effectiveness of Christ's sacrifice (10:5-10)

In contrast to what we have just read, the sacrifice of our Lord Jesus Christ at Golgotha was able to accomplish that which animal sacrifices could never do. How? Why? That is what the apostle now tells us:

> 10:5-7: 'To explain my point I must quote to you Psalm 40:6-8. These words, as all you Hebrews know, are Messianic. Think of what they are saying. They express what was in Christ's mind when he, the eternal Son of God, came into the world as Mary's child, the Son of Man.'

> 10:8: 'The Messiah recognises that God has no pleasure in the offerings and sacrifices laid down by the Old Testament law and still being offered at the time of his coming.'

> 10:9: 'He comes, then, not to offer those sacrifices, but to do God's will. He has no interest in the first. His whole purpose in coming into the world is to do the second.'

> 10:10: 'It is not by the way of animal sacrifices, but by the way of Christ's surrendering himself to do God's will, that men and women are set apart to belong to the Lord. It is not by animal sacrifices, but by Christ's voluntary offering of his body once for all, that redemption is accomplished.'

What the apostle is saying here is clear. God's will for the Messiah was that he should make a full atonement for sin. This necessitated sacrifice and the shedding of blood, and for this reason a body was prepared for him, that he might suffer. In his suffering and death the will of God was fully accomplished. In this way the second, or better, covenant came into operation.

Believers have been cleansed and set apart for God through the offering of the body of Jesus Christ, once for all. An atonement which perfectly pleases a holy God has been made. It was done this way, and not at all by animal sacrifices. The only effective atonement that there is lies in what Christ has done. It is not found anywhere else.

3. This point underlined and proved (10:11-18)

10:11: 'Think back again to Old Testament times. There was no seat in the Tabernacle, showing that there was no time to rest and that there was always work to be done. The work of offering sacrifices was never finished. As soon as the priest had done what he had to do, he had to do it again. This shows, as we have seen, that those sacrifices simply did not take away sin.'

10:12: 'How different it is with "this man", namely, Christ. He offered one sacrifice for sins, and only one. He did this "for ever", that is, as something that was never to be repeated. Then he sat down; his work was completed, finished, and over. But where did "this man" sit? It was not anywhere on earth, but "at the right hand of God".'

10:13: 'There he is, seated in the place of highest authority. He has no more battles to wage, no more temptations to endure, no further Gethsemane to experience, no new cross to be nailed to, no second tomb to be laid in. All his conflicts are over. He sits in triumph waiting for the day when all his enemies will be made his footstool (*Psa.* 110:1; *Phil:* 2:9-11). The next step for our Lord Jesus Christ will not be his repeating his sacrificial work; it will be his advent!'

10:14: 'His work is over, for by that single offering he perfected for ever those who have been set apart for God.'

The apostle is stressing that the whole of our salvation was accomplished at Calvary, and that there is nothing to add to what was done there. How unlike the experience of the Old Testament priests who, as soon as they had finished their offerings, had to start all over again! Their work was *never* finished.

10:15-17: 'The Holy Spirit, who is the ultimate author of Scripture, witnesses to this point in the statement that he makes in Jeremiah 31:33. There he speaks of the covenant that the death of Christ was to bring into operation, with its twin blessings of a transformed heart and a new record before God.'

10:18: 'Once this second blessing of entire and eternal forgiveness has been acquired, there just *cannot* be any further offering for sin. Once there has been a sufficient and effective sacrifice for sin, there can be no more sacrifice. Seeing that the whole price has been paid, what is there to pay for?'

Calvary ends all the sacrifices instituted in the Old Testament. They are now superfluous and unnecessary. They served well as shadows, pointing forward and dimly portraying what was to come. But they had no value beyond that, because they could not take away a single sin. Their time is over.

How firmly and strongly we must reject every idea that suggests that there are still sacrifices to be offered or re-offered. The Roman Catholic Church teaches that 'The Mass is not a mere remembrance of Calvary but the actual re-presentation of Christ's death, the continuation of His sacrifice and in itself that same sacrifice.'[2] In the light of the apostle's teaching in Hebrews, we can say that this is both a heresy and a blasphemy. By definition, no Christian church can have within it any place for priests, altars, or sacrifices.

It is easy, however, to point the finger at Rome. What shall we say of those within evangelical circles who teach that at some future time the Old Testament sacrifices will be offered again? It is true that they hold that 'these offerings will be memorial, looking back to the cross, as the offerings under the old covenant were anticipatory, looking forward to the cross.'[3] This is at best speculation, and at worst unashamed error. Christ himself has instituted a memorial of his death, which is to be observed until he returns. It is the Lord's Supper. Nothing else is needed or expected. Any return to priests, sacrifices, or Old Testament rites would be a massive act of disobedience, and would stand as an open denial of the fact that there is no place for the Old Covenant now that the New has come.

That said, let us now return more directly to Hebrews. The apostle has proved his case: Christ's work is infinitely superior to what the Hebrews were thinking of going back to. He is superior in his person. He is superior in his work. We need to ask, however, whether every reader fully realises the implications of what we have just been learning.

For example, is it possible that having read so far, there are still readers who are relying on something they think they can do in order to be accepted by God? Is it not at last clear to you that the only way to God is by relying on Christ's work, and that nothing else is necessary or required? Will you not at this point confess to God your foolishness, entrust yourself to Christ, and ask God to save you?

Or are there believers reading this book who can clearly see their sins, and who have consequently lost their peace and their sense of acceptance with God? Remember this: the Lord's acceptance of you has never been based on your performance, and therefore he will not reject you because of your poor performance. He accepts sinners on the basis of what *Christ* has done; and that work is perfect. Your sins are a disgrace, but do not get fixated upon them. Look away to Jesus Christ. Go on, consider him! Reflect again on his work. It is sinners that he reconciles to God, and nobody else.

The passage we have studied should convince us all again that it is a glorious thing to be a Christian! We have what we most need. How wonderful it is to know that all our sins have been forgiven! What peace of conscience we therefore enjoy. How privileged we are to be right with God, and to know this as we go through life, face the grave, and accelerate towards the final judgement. What

pleasure is ours as we remember that, because of Christ, God con-
siders us to be his friends and sons, and not to be his enemies!

There is no one like our Lord Jesus Christ. How awful, then, it
will be for the unforgiven millions to have to face him. He is their
Maker and their Judge, and his eternal anger against them will not
be removed unless they turn to him. But how tender he is with
those who do so! He receives them all and never turns them away.
They see something of his glories in this life and enter into all the
blessings of the New Covenant. They enjoy the promise of verse 17
and enter at last into heaven as pardoned sinners, blissfully singing
for ever the praises of the crucified Lamb, who is King of Kings
and Lord of Lords!

16

WHAT TO DO AND WHY

Please Read Hebrews 10:19-39

The New Covenant, brought into operation by Christ's death, actually does give the believer complete forgiveness and pardon for his sins. Christ's sacrifice and intercession actually do give the believing sinner access to the very presence of God, not in picture form, but in fact. Because of who Christ is, and what he has done, it is possible to go through life at peace with God, desiring him, knowing him, and enjoying fellowship with him. The Old Testament spoke of these privileges, but its rites and rituals brought no one to experience them. How different things are for those who have come to Christ!

These are the great truths that the apostle has been underlining and upon which he now builds. The passage before us is made up of three important movements:

1. What to do in the light of these truths: exhortation (10:19-25)

10:19: 'Let us take a few minutes to reflect on the facts that I have explained to you. We who are brothers in Christ have liberty, boldness and confidence to go into the holiest, that is, into the very presence of God, and not just into the shadow of things, like the Old Testament high priest did. God's holiness no longer excludes us from his presence. There is no need for us to cringe outside. We may go in, because the whole penalty that we deserve to bear was carried by Christ when he bled and died for us at the cross. We may enter. There is open access for every believer; *that* is our privilege!'

10:20: 'A new way, a living way, has been opened for us, and we may go right in. We come to God, not by means of a ceremony, a ritual, or a liturgy, but by a person! The veil no longer blocks us out, as it did in Old Testament times. At the same time as Christ's body was torn on the cross, the veil between God and man was torn, giving immediate access into God's presence. We, awful sinners that we are, may go in!'

10:21: 'The one who was sacrificed for us is also our high priest. We believers are his household, and he is the head of the house. The access we have, therefore, is not totally like that pictured in the tabernacle. There the high priest went in to the Holy of Holies, only to come out again almost immediately; but we go in to stay. There the access was limited to one man who went in once a year, but through Christ the way of access is open to all believers all of the time.'

10:22: 'Since the way is now freely open, let us avail ourselves of it! The facts being what they are, it is not only our privilege to draw near to God, but it is also our duty; otherwise we will be despising the work of Christ. Let us draw near—unhesitatingly, frequently, and intimately. Let us draw near—for praise, for thanksgiving, and to bring our requests. We are not in Old Testament days. There is nothing to keep us out, such as the ceremonial defilement, uncleansed consciences, and failure in ritual washing that excluded people in former times. Christ's blood has dealt with everything, so let us draw near with the fully formed assurance that the way to God really is open for us.'

10:23: 'This is not the time to loosen our grip, to waver in our faith, and to be tempted to go back to those Old Testament shadows that promised much but gave nothing. No, this is a time to hold fast. The Old Testament raised expectations, but it did not deliver. The New

Covenant is not like that. It will not let you down, because it has
been inaugurated by one who cannot lie.'

10:24-25: 'These things being so, this is not a time to be sowing
doubts in each other's minds and to be thinking of going back to
Judaism. On the contrary, it is a time to be stirring one another up
to ever greater degrees of Christian commitment. You should be
working out ways of doing it. You should be doing your very best to
increase each other's love and practical Christian living.

'You will never do this by absenting yourself from fellowship
with each other, as some of you have developed the habit of doing.
Flagging zeal and weakening faith are not healthy signs. Instead we
should all be recognising that we cannot live the Christian life on
our own. We should be meeting with each other as often as we can,
stirring one another up and encouraging one another.

'Very soon this present night will be over and a new day will
break. *That* day is nearer to us every day! That being so, every day
on earth should find us keener than the day before. *Today may be
the day when the Lord comes!* If it is, how ashamed I will be that I
have not lived this one day well; that I have not lived it better than
yesterday; and that I have not done my utmost to encourage and
help my fellow Christians to do the same!'

The apostle is making it clear that it is not enough to understand
the truth; there must be an appropriate response to it. The only
right response to what he has been explaining is an unashamed
Christian life characterised by prayer, fellowship, increasing zeal,
concern for the welfare of other believers, and constant expectancy
of the Lord's return. For myself, I find this deeply challenging, and
I can say the same for what comes next.

2. Where the road backward leads: warning (10:26-31)

10:26: 'For do not mistake what I am now going to say to you as, for
the fourth time in my letter, I give you a stern warning. If you have a

real understanding of gospel truth and embrace it, but then wilfully walk out on it, fully conscious of what you are doing, there will be dire consequences. If you deliberately reject the cross, do not think that atonement for your sins can be found elsewhere.'

It is important for us to see that the apostle is here talking about professing Christians who then forsake the faith, treat it as a lie and trample on what they once held dear. He is not talking about the sins and failures that all Christians experience. How can he be? He has already promised that weak believers can find grace to help, and failing Christians can find mercy, at the throne of grace (4:14-16). The gospel is full of tenderness. But it also speaks in the most severe tones to those who treat light as darkness.

This section is saying again what the three previous warning passages said: apostasy is something deliberate, and there is no way that such a sin can be covered. If you walk out on the Lord Jesus Christ, the only place that you can go to is outer darkness.

10:27: 'There is no way to have peace with God except by the way of the cross announced in the gospel message. So, if you turn your back on that, what awaits you is "a fearful expectation of judgment, and fiery indignation which will devour the adversaries". If you deliberately cease to be God's friend, you must be treated as his enemy.'

10:28: 'To reject the law that God gave through Moses was bad enough. Do you remember what happened to such people? If the offence was proved beyond dispute, they were always executed. No mercy was expected and none was given.'

10:29: 'If that was the certain penalty of breaking the law, how much greater will be the punishment for the sin of showing utter contempt for the Son of God, rejecting as worthless and unholy his blood-bought covenant which brought such a sanctifying transformation into your life, and despising the person and work of the Holy Spirit who brings God's grace into human lives?'

10:30-31: 'For the condition of apostasy there is no cure, and from the punishment for apostasy there is no escape. All that awaits such people is God's holy vengeance—the terrible prospect of falling into the hands of the living God as an unpardoned sinner who has set himself on a course of despising him!'

It is a wonderful thing to be a Christian and to experience and enjoy the blessings which the apostle has been speaking about. But it is an unspeakably awful thing to know the truth, to embrace it, to have true experiences of the Holy Spirit, but then to loosen your grip, to slip away, and finally to deliberately turn away from the Lord. The only safe course of action for a professing Christian, and the only happy one, is to make spiritual progress every day, as the apostle will now underline.

3. Where the road forward leads: encouragement (10:32-39)

10:32: 'Think back, right back to the earliest days of your Christian life, the days immediately following the day when the truth of the gospel burst like a great light into your mind. Those days were far from easy. They were days of trouble, of conflict, and of suffering.'

10:33: 'Everyone's eyes were on you. Some onlookers physically abused you, while others made you suffer by their words. That is not all. Even when hostility was not directed at you personally, you identified with and stood shoulder to shoulder with others who were going through such things.'

10:34: 'At that stage some, including me, were in prison for their faith. You showed sympathy with such prisoners and were not ashamed to identify yourselves with us. This led to your property being seized by your persecutors, but you accepted it joyfully.

'And how was it that you managed to put up with all this? Well, you were convinced, inwardly convinced, that whatever you may have lost on earth, you had better and more enduring possessions in heaven which could not be taken away from you. It was the sight of the Celestial City that kept you going!'

10:35: 'And that is right—the Christian life is not just for this earth. It leads us to our final destination, which is heaven. So do not throw away the settled faith that you have, which leads to such a glorious outcome and to such a great reward.'

10:36: 'Do not let your present temptations leads you away. What you need is not something visible and tangible, which you foolishly believe you can have by returning to the ineffective ordinances of the Old Testament. No, no; what you need right now is *stickability*, that is endurance and patience. You need the ability to keep going, so that when you have done God's will and stuck at doing what he wants, you may at last enter into the promised reward.

'In other words, your ruling desire should not be to turn back to an easier way. It should be to do what God wants. If you do, the reward will be yours!'

10:37: 'And remember, you do not have long to wait. In a very little while he who is coming *will* come. He will not come a moment later than planned. Despite all the difficulties you are experiencing, keep going. Hold out a little longer. Do not pack in now. Do not drop out of the race at this stage, and you will get safely home.'

10:38-39: 'Let me summarise what I have to say. Those who are *just* in the sight of God are men and women of faith. Those who live by faith, and die in faith, will certainly enter into the salvation secured for them by Christ. However, for those who shrink back, for those who retreat out of God's favour, there is nowhere for them to go, except into never-ending destruction.

'We are not in that category. We are those who believe and keep on believing. We go on and on in the life of faith and, at last, enter into eternity as saved souls.'

In this way, as we can see, the apostle has now become focussed on the theme of faith. For a while it is going to take up all his attention. In the next chapter, the famous eleventh chapter of Hebrews, he will tell us what faith is, how it displays itself and what are its rewards.

Before we move to that chapter, however, we need to be very sure that we have grasped what we have just been taught. Heaven is the destination of every believer. Nothing can keep a professing believer out of heaven, except the failure to persevere. Earlier chapters told us that the secret of perseverance is to expose ourselves to the Word of God and to constantly look away to our Lord Jesus Christ as our high priest. This overlaps with what we have just been taught about the importance of prayer, but we must also now add the dimensions of fellowship and daily expectation of the Lord's return.

How much we all need the warning of verse 38: 'Now the just shall live by faith; but if anyone draws back, my soul has no pleasure in him.'

How wonderful it would be if every reader of this book could then add from their heart verse 39: 'But we are not of those who draw back to perdition, but of those who believe to the saving of the soul'!

17

FAITH:
DEFINED AND ILLUSTRATED

Please Read Hebrews 11:1-16

We have learned that a true Christian is a person who, having come to Christ as the way to God, never finally walks out on him, despite many falls, failures, mistakes, and wanderings. Instead, he or she believes, and keeps on believing.

A true Christian is a man or woman of *faith*. But what is faith? What does a person who has faith look like? How does faith display itself? It is important that we should be able to answer such questions because, if we can, we will also be able to answer vital personal questions such as these: Do *I* have faith? Is my faith real? Is it a faith that will last throughout my life, support me in death, and carry me safely to heaven?

All our important questions about faith are answered in Hebrews chapter 11, of which we now study the first sixteen verses. This passage starts by answering our question about what faith is; we may call this paragraph *'Faith Defined'*. It then proceeds to answer our questions about how faith behaves; we may call that part *'Faith Illustrated'*.

1. What faith is: faith defined (11:1-3)

Faith is a sixth sense. By use of my five bodily senses I become sure of the reality of the physical world in which I live. I can see the flowers, touch them and smell them. I can taste my food and listen to my friends. But faith is not a bodily sense.

Faith is being sure of the unseen (verse 1b). We must be clear about this. It is not being sure of the *unknown*, but of the *unseen*. These unseen things fall into two categories.

First of all, some things are unseen because they have not happened yet, or because I have not yet arrived where they are. For example, God's Word promises me and every other believer that we will immediately and fully enjoy Christ's company from the very moment that we die. It promises me a resurrection body like Christ's glorious body. It promises me acquittal at the final judgement, a home in heaven, and the full enjoying of God throughout eternity. I am sure that I will receive all these blessings, because God has promised them. He has given his word. 'Faith is being sure of what we hope for' (verse 1a, NIV).[1]

Secondly, some things are unseen because they cannot be seen. This is supremely true of God, but is also true of the whole spiritual world. Like all believers, I am sure that God exists, and that the God who exists is the God of the Bible. I am also sure of the existence of angels and demons. My confidence is built on what God has revealed in his Word and, being sure of the reality of these things, I take them all into account in my thoughts, words and actions. Faith is being 'certain of what we do not see' (verse 1b, NIV).

There are, then, two aspects to faith. I am sure of the unseen in two ways. My certainty in both cases, however, is built on the same foundation: God has spoken and I believe what he has said. These things are realities to me. They are not less real, but more real! We believers are confident of what we hope for and convinced of what we do not see (verse 1)

11:2: 'In a few moments I am going to take you on a tour of some great people of Old Testament days. What did they all have in common? What did they have which meant that they enjoyed the favour and smile of God? It was *faith*, which I have just defined.'

11:3: 'They lived in the same physical universe as we do. All its inhabitants believe that it exists, but where did it come from? Some believe that it just "happened", while others believe that it has always been here in some shape or form. We know better. We know that it was all formed by God, who spoke it into existence. It was made out of nothing by an act of almighty power. There is a Creator to whom we are all answerable. Of this we are sure. We have no doubts about it, but why not? We have come to this certainty by faith and not by observation, because, of course, no human was around to see it all happening.'

It is clear, then, what faith is; and we can now be equally clear in knowing whether we have it or not. However, the apostle has previously told us that only those who live by faith, and who die in faith, arrive at their heavenly reward. Have any such men and women ever existed? He has just mentioned, in a general way, the people of old who lived and died in God's favour (verse 2); but who, in particular, did he have in his mind?

He will now give us a list of such people. He will show to us that they were sure in the two ways that we have mentioned, and that they took both future and unseen realities into account in the way that they lived. He will illustrate faith by referring to various Old Testament characters and, in doing so, he will show us how faith behaves.

2. How faith behaves: faith illustrated (11:14-16)

Abel (verse 4)

The invisible God was a reality to Abel and he desired to approach him. From instructions that are not recorded in the Old Testament, but which had obviously been given, Abel knew that he could not come as he was. He would have to come by the way of sacrifice and blood atonement, typifying (as we have seen) the coming great sacrifice, Christ.

Nobody had come to God in worship before, and Abel had nothing but God's word to guide him as to how he should do it. He acted in obedience to God's bare word and was accepted. His brother Cain, however, chose a different path, presumably because he thought that he knew better. Ignoring God's instructions, he invented his own way to come in worship, only to see his offering refused.

Abel proves that those who come to God by the way of faith are accepted by God, and that all others are turned away. In this way he still speaks to us. We are to take note of the lesson. We must take God's Word at its face value and act in line with what he has said.

Enoch (verses 5-6)

Enoch lived at a time when almost everyone was intent on pleasing himself. To him the eternal God was a reality and he was therefore intent on pleasing *him*. He walked and talked with God, and one day walked with him to his house without ever coming back. He arrived there without dying and did not leave his body behind!

The invisible realm was the supreme reality to Enoch, and if we would please God today, that is still the way that it has got to be. We have to be certain that he is, and that he is worth walking with. Faith is being convinced of the reality of the unseen, on the ground of what God has revealed in his Word. The person who has true faith can nurse only one ambition, and that is to please God. Nothing else can possibly be more important. That is how faith behaves.

Noah (verse 7)

Now let us look at Noah. He grew up in a world where it had never rained, so how did he know that it would? He knew it because God had told him and he believed it to be true, although there was no possible evidence he could muster as proof. Acting on the unseen truth, and moved with fear, he spent a century building the ark by which he and his family would eventually be saved.

What an example he was of believing, believing, and continuing to believe! Other people mocked and jested, saying that it could never happen. Noah took God at his Word and acted accordingly. In the end, his faith was vindicated, and the surrounding world was shown up for what it was—anti-God and unbelieving. But Noah also was shown up for what he was—a man who had come into the experience of being accepted and approved by God *through faith*.

Abraham (verses 8-10)

There is no greater example of faith than Abraham. He left his own country and went off into the unknown, with nothing to rely on except that God had told him to go and had promised him an inheritance.

The invisible God was so real to him, and his word so sure, that Abraham did not hesitate to obey. He left what others called 'certainties' for what they call 'uncertainties'. But he did not see things that way. This was because he was a man of faith and God's word was therefore surer to him than anything else.

That is why he put up with living in tents through all those years. God had given him a promise, which was later repeated to Isaac, and then to Jacob. They were to enter into an inheritance. This consisted of something much better and more enduring than what the land of Canaan could offer. They were certain to enter into that inheritance. All that they had to do was what God told them.

Sarah (verses 11-12)[2]

Sarah, Abraham's wife, displayed the same faith. She had her doubts, but her faith was real. She came to an age when she was far too old to have a child. It was a clear impossibility. But she believed that she would and duly conceived, on no other ground except the fact that God had promised it.

This was the way that an old man, himself also as good as dead, became the ancestor of an innumerable company. Yes, if Abraham had not had enduring faith, the Jewish nation would never have come into existence. What a rebuke the apostle thus gives to the believing Jews who were now thinking of giving up their faith in favour of something more 'Jewish'!

Living in true faith means dying in faith (verse 13-16)

These people lived and behaved as they did because the invisible God and the invisible realm were real to them, and because they took God at his word. But in this life they did not see or experience all that God had promised them. They did not live to see the Messiah or to witness the better sacrifice, nor did they enter into their promised inheritance and dwelling-place. This does not alter the fact that they *saw* all these things at a distance, knew them to be certain, and set their hearts on them. Not only so, but they told the people around them that they did not belong *here,* for *those things* were what they lived for and which were close to their hearts.

If you had asked any of them what they were after in this life, they would have given you the same answer. They were seeking their homeland (verse 14). Its reality loomed so large in their thinking that it never crossed their minds to live like everybody else. Nor did they have any desire to go back to what they were before, although they had every opportunity to do so. All their hearts and hopes were set on getting safely into God's dwelling-place, into heaven.

What, above all else, was most real to them? It was God, the invisible God. What, above all else, were they sure of? It was that God's word is true and trustworthy, and that it is therefore a certainty that eternal glory is waiting for those who walk with him.

God, seeing them believing and acting like this, was and is actually proud of them! He is not ashamed to be their God. He is delighted with them; he takes pleasure in them. He has indeed prepared for them what they were seeking, and not one of them will be disappointed. We shall see those Old Testament saints in heaven. They lived in faith and they died in faith, so it is certain. That is the main lesson this passage is trying to teach the Hebrews—and us!

May I, as the author of this book you are reading, ask you some more questions at this point? Do you have faith? Is the invisible God a reality to you? Do you regard his Word as sure?

In turn, does this lead you to approach him in the way that he has appointed (as Abel did)? Does it move you to see that pleasing him is the most important thing in the world (as Enoch saw)? Does it inspire you to obey him, even when it seems that you might be throwing everything away (as Abraham obeyed)? Does it push you to trust that what he says will happen, even though it seems impossible (as Sarah trusted)?

Do you have faith? Are you staking your life, your death, and your eternity on what God has said? If you are, you will not be disappointed or let down. Nor is he ashamed to be your God, or to walk with you in this life, or to welcome you into his home in the next. But the reverse is also true, and horribly so. If you do not have faith, and will not have faith, there is nowhere for you to go, except to live and die under his anger, and to go into eternal lostness. The Epistle to the Hebrews, and chapter 11 in particular, has been written so that you might see that this does not have to be the case.

18

NOTHING CAN EXTINGUISH TRUE FAITH

PLEASE READ HEBREWS 11:17-40

At this point in his letter, the apostle is focussing on the subject of faith. He has been explaining what it is and how it behaves. However, we must not forget that he is writing to men and women who are seriously thinking of walking out on their faith. This being so, there is a particular point that he now wants to stress: true faith never dies out. There is nothing that can extinguish it. This is the solitary lesson that occupies the remainder of chapter 11, and the apostle teaches it by stressing two truths:

1. Faith looks forward when there is nothing to look forward to (11:17-28)

Take the case of Abraham (verses 17-19)

On more than one occasion God had told Abraham that he would have a great number of descendants, and one very special one. He had made it clear that these promises would be fulfilled through his son Isaac. Abraham took God at his word. He did not doubt that it would all come true.

At this point God told Abraham to sacrifice Isaac. Now Abraham had a problem on his hands, but once he had thought everything through he came to a clear conclusion. God could not break his word and let him down; of that he was sure. So then, if God had promised him descendants through Isaac, whom he now had to kill, it could only mean that God was planning to raise Isaac from the dead! Figuratively speaking, of course, that is exactly what happened. The big point, however, is this: at a time in human history when there had never been a single instance of a dead person coming back to life, Abraham concluded that that was exactly what was going to happen!

God cannot break his word. So when, humanly speaking, there was nothing to look forward to, Abraham looked forward to Isaac's resurrection! That is how true faith behaves. Nothing can extinguish it. It never moves from its conviction that God's word is to be trusted. What a rebuke this was to the Hebrews!

Take the case of Isaac (verse 20)

The time came when Isaac was an old man who was coming to the end of his days. People near the end of their life tend to spend their time looking back, because they see nothing ahead. But in his advancing years, what was Isaac doing? He was looking forward! His mind was on 'things to come' (verse 20).

Although he found out that he had been the victim of deceit and trickery, the old man was unwilling to withdraw what he had said about the respective futures of his sons Jacob and Esau: God's purposes would be carried forward by Jacob, and Esau was to have no place in them, although he would know some earthly blessings during his lifetime. Isaac had taken it for granted that Esau, his older son, would be God's chosen instrument for the future. Although Jacob's tactics were sinful and wrong, Isaac could now see that the blessing he had given him was God's will. The covenant promises given to Abraham would be fulfilled through Jacob's line. He was unshakeably sure of it, although he was never to see it for himself. That is faith.

Take the case of Jacob (verse 21)

When Jacob was almost at the point of death, he blessed his two grandsons whom their father Joseph had brought to his bed-side. As he did so, he had a great awareness of the presence of the invisible God. He predicted the future of each boy and dis-played his certainty as to how the purposes of God would proceed through each one. He had only a few moments left on earth, yet he was still looking forward. God was a reality and his word was sure. How few old people enjoy *that* perspective; but that is how faith behaves.

Take the case of Joseph (verse 22)

During his wonderful life, Joseph had passed through a great variety of different experiences, and yet, in his last moments, even he was still looking forward! Although there was no sign of it at the time, he could see the coming Exodus. God had promised that the Israelites would eventually leave Egypt. Joseph had not lived to see it, but he knew that it was definitely going to happen. This being so, he gave clear instructions about what was to be done with his bones: they were not to remain in Egypt, but were to accom-pany Israel to the promised land, to have their final burial there.

Like the others we have mentioned, Joseph lived and died with-out seeing all that God had promised. But this did not make him cynical, or fill him with doubts and hesitations. What God had promised would certainly happen—no other possibility crossed his mind. That great conviction ruled both the way that he lived and the way that he died. Even when humanly speaking he 'had it all' and there was nothing left to look forward to, even then he looked forward. That is what genuine faith does.

Take the case of Moses (verses 23-28)

At a time when there was no future for Hebrew boys, Moses' parents knew differently and looked forward (verse 23). They could see that their newborn son was no ordinary child and that God had a special rôle for him. Without any fear of Pharaoh's command to exterminate infant sons, they hid him for three months, waiting for God's purpose to work itself out.

At a time when there was no future outside the Egyptian royal court, Moses knew differently (verses 24-26). He could see that the long-term future lay with the people of God and the kingdom of Christ, and not with the sinful environment that surrounded him. He therefore chose to throw in his lot with Israel and not with Egypt; to enjoy the eternal reward and not to enjoy the temporary treasures and passing pleasures of the hour.

The invisible God was more real to Moses than the dictator of an earthly super-power, and so he showed no fear when he had to confront that dictator with demands that the Hebrews should be released from their slavery (verse 27). And later, when furious Pharaoh's pursuing armies seemed certain to obliterate escaping Israel, Moses still showed no fear and looked forward. Conquered by the reality of God and the integrity of his promises, nothing could break him. The same spirit had permeated the original Passover, the night before Israel left (verse 28). It was a looking forward, based on God's word, which (of course!) was not disappointed.

How different men and women of faith are from other people! All these examples bear this out. Ordinary men and women base their thoughts about the future on what they see, what they hope for, what they plan, and what they think is possible or feasible.

Believers are not like that at all. All their thoughts about the future are regulated by the promises of God. They view everything in the light of what his Word teaches. And so, when the world has nothing to look forward to, the Christian *does!* In his mind's eye he gets excited about the continuing progress of the gospel, the return of his Lord, the ruin of Satan, the acquittal of the final judgement, and the wonder of being with Christ eternally.

The uncrushed optimism of the believer is not based on anything that can be seen. The existence of these future realities cannot be 'proved' in any normal sense. The lack of 'evidence' causes the unbelieving world to question whether anything in the Christian's hope can be true, or even to mock the idea. The believer continues to believe, quite undeterred. He is sure of what God has promised. It is not open to question, and his certainty brings him calm comfort and excited expectancy. There is nothing as sure as God's Word, and so he does not give in to pessimism, despair, or apostasy. The future is always as bright as the promises of God!

May I ask you if you live like that? Are all your views of the future governed by what God has said? Do you really have faith? Oh, what joy there is in being a believer! When everyone else's world is collapsing, ours has hardly begun!

2. Faith keeps going when everything else gives up (11:29-40)

Look what happened at the Red Sea (verse 29)

As they stood on the shores of the Red Sea, Moses and the escaping Israelites knew that God was with them and that he had promised to see them safely across. That is faith; what else could have kept them going in that situation?

The crossing of the Red Sea seemed impossible. It was against reason. With Pharaoh's armies approaching, the reality was that they were trapped and that they were facing certain death. But faith does not die in such situations. The Israelites took God at his word and acted on the assumption that he was with them. By the next morning they were all safe and sound on the other side, unlike the drowned Egyptians, who were devoid of faith. Not even difficulties kill genuine faith. Come what may, it keeps going. What a rebuke this must have been to the first readers of Hebrews, who were on the brink of apostasy.

Look what happened at Jericho (verses 30-31)

When the Israelites came at last to the Promised Land, the first enemy city they had to conquer was Jericho. Once a day, for six days, they marched around it. Nothing happened; so why did they keep going? The answer is that they believed what God had said and obeyed his instructions to the letter. Faith kept going and did not peter out: it gave the victory shout, saw the walls fall flat, and soon completed the conquest.

And have you ever put yourself in the shoes of Rahab? She lived on the wall, and yet God had determined that the wall was to fall down! She was a native of Jericho, and God had said that all the native population was to perish. But did she cry, 'It's all up with me!'? No; her faith remained intact. In God's name, the Hebrew spies had given her a promise. She believed it. She had a continuous awareness of the reality and trustworthiness of God which never left her, even in the supposedly impossible circumstances in which she found herself. Faith keeps going. If it is genuine, nothing can extinguish it.

Look at the whole history of Israel (verses 32-38)

Here the apostle admits that he simply does not have enough time to mention every example of faith to be found in the Scriptures and history of the Hebrews to whom he is writing. The point they must grasp is that *all* the great heroes of their nation were so because they were people of faith. That is how they did what they did.

And what did they do? They performed great acts of courage, valour, bravery, boldness, and endurance. In persecution, they withstood pain and torture. They knew everything there is to know about personal sacrifice. The apostle spells it out briefly and comprehensively in verses 33-38, where the whole history of Israel is summarised in a few brief sentences. By searching the Old Testament it is not hard to discover many of the events referred to here.

When everything was against them, these men and women remained true to the Lord—unlike the Hebrews to whom the apostle is writing! What was their secret? They had faith. God was real to them. They were certain that his word was true; that what he had said would happen *would* happen; that what he had promised them would be theirs. They were more sure of this than of anything. And so they never gave up, they never gave in, they never went back to what they were before, they never walked out on their God, and they never lived in the same way as others.

That is how true faith behaves. When everything is hopeless and everyone has given up, it keeps going. 'God is real and his Word is true' is its root conviction, and it acts in the light of this conviction, whatever the cost may be. How can it do otherwise?

Look at those Old Testament believers once again (verses 39-40)

They lived by faith, and God smiled on them. And that, also, is how they died. Despite all the promises given to them, they never saw the Messiah on earth, they never witnessed the perfect sacrifice and never set their eyes on the glorious city they were seeking. They never actually held in their hands any of the things they had set their heart on.

They were not allowed to do it because they had to wait for us. Those Old Testament days were not superior, (as the original readers of Hebrews seemed to be thinking), but inferior. It was not God's will that they should enter into everything that they longed for, and then that we New Testament believers should come along as a sort of afterthought, as second-rate children of God.

We have seen what they never saw; some New Testament believers saw Christ and his cross with their own eyes, and the rest of us can look back on his incarnation, life, ministry, death and resurrection. But none of us—whether we are believers of the Old Testament or the New—has yet seen the promised city. We shall enter that together, all at the same time, with no one going in front of the other. Old Testament believers had their hearts set on heaven, and so do we. We shall arrive in heaven hand in hand.

What is necessary, then, is not a return to Old Testament ceremonies and rituals (as the original readers were thinking), but that we should have genuine faith. Only men and women of faith will be in heaven. Quite frankly, those who renounce their faith, or allow it to wither away, will not be there. Fortunately, nothing can extinguish true faith. Nothing!

None of us should dare to leave this great chapter without once more asking whether we have faith. Is the invisible world real to me? Am I sure of God's Word – sufficiently sure of it to obey it, and to rely on the Christ it proclaims for my eternal salvation?

The final proof that my faith is real will be that it is still with me when I die. In my dying moments I will still be looking forward. When all else has left me—even my last remnants of health and consciousness—faith will remain.

It is time for all of us to put away everything that hinders our progress in faith. This is precisely the note that the apostle will sound next, as he opens chapter 12.

19

RUN THE RACE,
LOOKING UNTO JESUS

Please Read Hebrews 12:1-4

In our studies in Hebrews we come now to 12:1-4. The Hebrews in question, you will remember, were Jews who had become Christians, but who were now thinking of giving it all up and going back to Judaism. On several occasions the apostle has warned them not to do that because, if they do, they will be lost. The Lord Jesus Christ is uniquely superior, both in who he is and what he has done. Those who turn their back on him have only one place to go—into outer darkness.

The only safe course for a professing Christian is to go on, and on, and on, in the faith. People who have genuine faith live by that faith and die in it too. Nothing can extinguish it. The apostle has illustrated this by referring to a number of men and women mentioned in the Old Testament.

All this is what is in the readers' minds as they now read the apostle's 'Therefore . . .'—in other words: 'In the light of what I have said already, I have something further to say to you.' What he has to say consists of a vivid picture and three rules.

1. A vivid picture (12:1)

We are at the Olympic Games, in an immense stadium crowded with people. Races are being run. Again and again we watch as athletes come onto the track. If it were today, we would see them take off their track suits to reveal their minimal running kit underneath. But it is not today; it is the first century A.D. If an athlete were to run with his belt on it would weigh him down and impede his progress; so off it comes. If he were to run in his cloak, it would soon wrap around him and trip him up; so off that comes too. In fact, first-century athletes ran without a stitch on. There was nothing to get in the way.

Race after race takes place. Each one is long and difficult. We see an athlete panting and tempted to drop out, but he keeps going, for in these Christian games there are prizes for all who reach the tape, not just for the one who finishes first.

Again and again we see the runners tempted to give up through weariness or because they feel faint. But do they stop? No; they go on, and on, and on. At last each one crosses the finishing line and enters into his reward.

Those who finish take their place in the stands, and remain there to watch those who are still running, or will run next. Each one who runs does so in the knowledge that he is observed and surrounded by those who have already successfully finished. This spurs him on to do his best, to complete the race, and not to drop out, so that he can enter into his reward as well. He knows that he is not facing anything that the spectators have not already faced. If he keeps going he must and will experience what they are now enjoying; it is certain.

And now it is *our* turn to take to the track. All eyes are on us. No one else is running at the moment but us. All those who have successfully lived and died in the faith are watching us, as also is the one who chose us to run the race, who ran it perfectly himself, and who is now standing at the finishing line.

Shall we now drop out—we who are only facing difficulties that others have faced before us? Are we going to falter, to leave the track, to give up, and to walk away? Are we going to fail in the race for which we have been entered?

That is what the Hebrews were on the verge of doing as, without doubt, some readers are too. How can we keep going? What is the secret of running the race well and safely arriving at the finish? What is the secret of doing well in the Christian life, of keeping going in the life of faith, and of not apostatising and being lost? This is what the apostle is now going to tell us.

It is vitally important that we take his teaching to heart. These few verses show the difference between keeping going and entering into our heavenly reward, and dropping out and being lost.

2. Three rules (12:1-4)

I am writing a book. If I were not, but was preaching to a congregation, I would look each person in the eyes and solemnly charge them to listen to God's Word in these verses, and to close their ears to what other voices are saying.

Standing on the touchline are people who are shouting to us, telling us that we will never get anywhere in the Christian life *'unless . . .'* They forcefully warn us that all real progress is impossible *unless* we receive the baptism of the Holy Spirit, or *unless* we are sealed by the Holy Spirit, or *unless* we are fully consecrated to the Lord, or experience a revival, or pass through a crisis by which our 'old man' dies, *etc.* The terminology changes, but the message is always the same: we will get nowhere in the Christian life unless we have some sort of memorable special experience, quite distinct from our conversion.

I plead with my readers to listen to God's Word and not to these voices. Here are three rules, apostolic rules, for successfully living and dying in the faith. Here are three rules for running the race which will prevent us from dropping out, failing to reach the tape, and losing the promised reward.

(i.) *Strip for action* (verse 1)

If you run in a cloak it will soon get in the way. It will wrap around you, trap you and trip you. Take it off! In the same way, get rid of all sin in your life. Finish with it. Do not think that you can hold on to anything you know to be sinful and, at the same time, run the race well. At best it will slow you down, and at worst it will cause you to stumble and leave the track. This is not an area where Christians have a right to differ. All that breaks the Ten Commandments or does not reflect their spirit, all that is not in line with God's Word, all that is unlike the character of our Lord Jesus Christ, is sin. Give it up. The more attached you are to it, the more important it is that you get it out of your life.

But that is not all. Even before the apostle mentions 'the sin which so easily ensnares us' he refers to laying aside 'every weight'. Some things are not wrong in themselves, but they hinder my spiritual effectiveness, weaken my faith, dampen my zeal, reduce my power to resist temptation, and tend to enslave me. These things must be laid aside. Everything that hinders my spiritual progress must be thrown away. Such things are not necessarily low or vulgar; they may be beautiful, intellectual, and noble. In the lives of certain believers, we may be talking about a sport, a hobby, a leisure pursuit, a job, a course of study, an ambition, a place, a friendship, or any number of legitimate interests or experiences. It does not matter what it is; if it gets in the way of my progress in the Christian life, it must go. And it must go *now!*

Those who are determined to run well, without exception, strip for action. If a Christian has poor knowledge, a life that does not reflect Christ, and a tepid heart, it is not because they are the victim of their environment or because some special experience has not yet come their way. It is because something is impeding their progress and they have not yet put it away. They need to find out what it is and sort it out, and they need to do that *today!*

(ii.) *Learn to say 'Come what may'* (1b)

The Christian life is not an easy stroll; so the apostle says 'run'. There are many difficulties along the way, and every one of us is sometimes tempted to drop out; so the apostle says 'with endurance'. The path we are on is not one of our own choosing, but has been marked out for us; so the apostle talks of 'the race that is set before us'.

If you have ever done any cross-country running, it is not something that you will easily forget. For many of us, it is one of the less pleasant memories of our school days. Even now we wince when we think of the legs that were as heavy as lead, the lungs that were paining and burning, and that unique throbbing in the temples. Then, when you feel completely exhausted, you find that there is still a gate to vault, a ditch to jump, a stream to wade through, and many more miles than you expected! In such races there is only one thing that stops you dropping out; it is the determination to keep going *come what may*. We understood all too easily why the apostle tells us to 'run with endurance'.

There is only one way to keep going in the life of faith and to enter into the promised reward. It is the state of mind which says, 'Whatever happens . . . however I feel . . . whether I am on my own or in company . . . even if I am laughed at . . . even if it costs me everything . . . I will keep going, *come what may.'* And you will! You will receive strength from above. Such determination is what it means to deny yourself, to take up your cross daily and to follow him (*Luke* 9:23-26).

(iii.) *Look to Jesus . . . consider him* (verses 2a, 3a)

In this third rule the apostle is saying yet again what he has been telling his readers throughout his letter. They are being tempted to go back to the Old Testament priesthood, sacrifices, and tabernacle, so he has shown them that the priesthood, sacrifice, and tabernacle of our Lord Jesus Christ are infinitely better. If they fix their eyes on him and see him clearly, they will never want to go back to those other things.

All Christians today are constantly bombarded with messages and influences which announce that a life lived without Christ is actually quite attractive. If they spent time having a good look at him, they would never want to go back to such a life. Look, look at who he is, at what he has done, and what he gives sinners in this life, at what he will give them at death, at the resurrection, at the judgement and in eternity!

The apostle now gives us three reasons for focussing our attention on him and always keeping him in mind:

(a.) From him our faith comes, and by him it is sustained to the end (verse 2a)

It is half a century since I left school, but my memories of Tom Clamp are as fresh as ever. He had spent his earlier years as a sergeant-instructor in the army, ensuring that troops were in tip-top condition physically. In middle life he switched to being a gym master and to imposing military standards on teenage boys! He never asked us to do anything easy. Every lesson was hard and sometimes there were tears. And yet we loved him—to his very bones!

Tom Clamp entered us for long cross-country races but, as we ran the difficult course, he would keep popping up at key places in order to spur us on. To this day, I do not know how he did it. Not only so, but when we eventually got to the finish, there he was again, encouraging us through the final yards, welcoming us at the line, and congratulating us afterwards. We ran well for him.

How different he was from some other gym teachers! They entered us for races, never appeared during the course, and were absent at the end. After those races we wandered round the changing-rooms lonely, bewildered, exhausted, and discouraged. None of us had run well.

It is our Lord who has entered us into the life of faith, it is he who welcomes us at the end, and it is he who accompanies us throughout every stride of the race, and not just at its key points. Look at him (in his Word). Consider him (in sustained thought and meditation). Those who look for him, focus on him, and listen to him always run well. Put him out of your minds, however, and you will soon find that you are out of the race.

(b.) Learn from his example (verse 2b)

Jesus himself has run the race you are running—the life of faith. What kept *him* going? What was the outcome for *him?* Everyone else who has run this race has done so defectively. He is the only one who has ever run it perfectly. For him, it meant going through the unspeakable pain of the cross and all the shame that went with it. But he looked forward. He looked upwards. He never lost sight of where the road would lead and the joy that would at last be his. The difficulties were infinite. The temptation to give up was, humanly speaking, unbearable. But it was not on these that he fixed his attention. He never lost sight of the goal, and at last he sat down at the right hand of the throne of God. It is in that place of highest honour that he still sits.

(c.) Appreciate what will happen to you if you do not look, to him (verses 3-4)

Turn your eyes away from everything else and look at him. Look at him. You are surrounded by enemies. You experience open hostility and hatred and, in some cases, there are those who are plotting your murder. Murder? Yes, that is something that he faced, which you have not yet had to face in your battle with sin.

But it may come to you. And when it comes to you, or anything else similarly difficult, you will give up, unless your eyes are fixed squarely on Jesus Christ.

The words of verse 3 suggest that giving up may take place in one of two ways. Some people leave the race through sudden collapse. Others experience a gradual breakdown of stamina; little by little they lose strength until they drop out. One is as dangerous as the other, because both lead to people dropping out of the race completely.

Two simple alternatives present themselves to all of us who profess to follow Christ: we either have clear views of him and keep close to him, or we drop out of the race altogether and proceed to eternal ruin. The example of other believers may spur us on, but, in the long run, even that will not keep us going. In the final analysis, everything depends on us stripping for action and declaring war on sin and all that is spiritually unhelpful. For this to happen, we must determine that we will go forward spiritually *come what may*. This requires us to keep close to the Lord Jesus Christ, whom we keep constantly in mind, whose example we follow, and whose strength we constantly call upon.

I am running the race, but will I finish it? Will I take my place in the stands? Will I be present with all men and women of faith—past, present and future—at the prize-giving? Or will I slacken off, slow down, and finally drop out, thus never reaching the finish and never enjoying the reward?

These eternal issues will be decided by whether or not I really take to heart Hebrews 12:1-4.

20

CHASTISEMENT AND ENCOURAGEMENT

PLEASE READ HEBREWS 12:5-17

The apostle has just given his readers three important rules. Taking them to heart is the difference between continuing in the life of faith and entering into the eternal reward, and dropping out of the race and being lost.

'Very well', says somebody, 'But I don't understand *why* there have to be all these difficulties in the Christian life. Every step of the way there are temptations, setbacks, opposition, problems, and pains. Why can't it all be easy?'

It is because they did not know the answer to this question that the Hebrews were seriously thinking of giving up and dropping out. This being the case, the apostle changes his illustration from that of a race to that of a family. With this picture in mind he proceeds at once to answer the perplexing question.

1. Why there have to be difficulties in the Christian life (12:5-11)

12:5-6: 'The reason that you are in this perplexity is because you have forgotten the Book of Proverbs. Do you not remember what is written in Proverbs 3:11-12?'

12:7: 'Let me explain what I mean. God has brought into your lives all sorts of painful experiences. They are not accidents; they are acts of God. Your Heavenly Father actually hurts his children!

'When he does this, it is because he is dealing with you as sons. Have you ever heard of a son who his father did *not* chastise? All of you who have any experience of family life know that rebuke and punishment are just as much part of a parent's love as are cuddling and embracing.'

12:8: 'It is by the discipline, training, and chastisement of our fathers that we are acknowledged as true sons. God is a perfect Father, and we can be certain that he will treat all his children in a fatherly manner, with no exceptions. If you claim to be his child, but have no painful experiences brought into your life by him, there can be only one explanation—you are a spurious son; he does not accept you as his child. That is why there are painful experiences in the Christian life. It is a proof of sonship!'

The apostle's teaching is very easy to follow. All of us know that if one of our children deliberately broke a neighbour's window, we would deal with the child appropriately. However, if a neighbour's child does something similar, we impose no sanctions whatever. Why not? It is because one child is ours and the other is not. We only chastise the children who are ours. We love them, and we love for their good, in a way that we do not love the children of others.

All experienced parents know that a loving spanking is as much a sign of total acceptance as the fondest cuddle at bedtime. In the same way we give our children tasks to do, not all of which are easy. As time goes by, we expect our children to carry increasing responsibility appropriate to their age, and sometimes this proves to be very difficult for them. This is part and parcel of the training and discipline that we give them to prepare them for adult life. We would not do it if we did not love them. The pains they go through are proofs of our care!

12:9: 'Now then, since we have had earthly fathers who corrected us, it should not surprise us that our Heavenly Father does the same. And what attitude did our earthly father's correction instil in us? It inspired respect. He restrained our rebellion and brought us at last to honour him. If he had not done this we would have lived as we pleased—and in our hearts we would have despised him for being "soft".

'If that is the effect that *that* discipline had upon us, how much more should it be the case when our heavenly Father disciplines us? Earthly discipline did us good. His discipline, therefore, is not something to kick against, to grumble about, or to resent. It is something to submit to. We should receive it with appreciation. It is intended for our good, and by learning from it we not only learn how to live and to avoid fatal mistakes—it actually brings us to life!'

12:10-11: 'There are however differences between the two disciplines. Our earthly fathers imposed their discipline and training on us for only a short time. Their discipline was not perfect, and sometimes they exercised it for their own ends (because they had been inconvenienced, embarrassed, or simply because they wanted some "peace and quiet"). God's discipline is not like that. It is always exercised for our benefit. It is never selfish. Its sole intention *every time* is that our characters may be like his—holy.

'Mind you, whether it is imposed by an earthly father or a heavenly one, no discipline is appreciated at the time. The child often reacts with resentment, accusation ("You don't love me!"), or tears. But its final results make it more than worthwhile. In those who have been trained by it, "it yields the peaceable fruit of righteousness". They become people who treat others correctly, who live at peace with them, and who live by a set of right values. That is also what God's discipline does and that is why we must not resent it.'

We are not to despise the Lord's discipline (verse 5) or to lose heart when it comes our way (verse 5b). Instead, we are to submit to it (verse 9b) and to see it as convincing proof that he accepts us as his children (verse 7), for whom he intends nothing but good.

In particular, we are to see that he has designed it to develop in us a holy character (verses 10b-11).

I am sure that all readers will agree that this is a very challenging paragraph. We now understand why there have to be difficulties in the Christian life. So how do we react to hard experiences? How do we greet persecution, illness, disappointments, setbacks, and trouble? If we take this teaching to heart, we will never be able to see these things in the same way again. Its effect on our lives will be obvious. It is this point that the apostle now pursues.

2. The effects that this teaching should have on our lives (12:12-17)

God's chastening should have three effects on our lives. To bring this home to us, we now leave the picture of the family and return to that of the athletes given in 12:1-4.

(i.) *Do not give in to discouragement* (verses 12-13)

12:12: 'As I write you are still running the race, but only just. The going is hard, the difficulties cannot be numbered, and your pains are increasing. You are on the verge of giving up. Your hands are hanging down. The spring has gone out of your step. Your legs are sagging.

'Lift those hands up! Straighten up! Take heart; all these difficulties are not intended to ruin you, but to make you into the man or woman that God wants you to be. You have a choice: you can resent them and give up, or you can take them for what God has sent them to be.

12:13: 'There you are wobbling, and getting dangerously near to zig-zagging off the track. Stop it and run straight ahead! You have begun to shuffle, to limp, and to be half-hearted in your Christian life. If you continue like that you will soon twist your ankle, dislocate something, or give yourself a sprain. That really will be the end of your race.

'Instead of that, shake off this defeatism that has got hold of you. Run properly. Find your pace again. This is not a time to give in to discouragement. No, no; instead let your present difficulties cause you to pull yourself together and to renew your determination. Keep going and the endangered ankle will soon be all right again; very soon you will once more be running as you should.'

There are only two attitudes to trouble. One will ruin us and one will strengthen us. Which will be ours? Persecution, illness, frustrations, and misunderstandings hit us all, as do a thousand other heartaches. The theory has to be worked out in practice. From now on, which mindset will be ours?

(ii.) *Sprint forward* (verse 14)

'What is paining you at the moment? Do not see this as a time to give up and to drop out. See it instead as a time to make a sprint. Your trial has been sent to do you good, so make up your mind to profit from it. Determine that as it has been sent to advance you in holiness, you will use it to do just that. It is there to bless you, not to ruin you. Do not treat it as a cruel master but as a willing servant. Yes, use this time to make a sprint.

'There are two particular issues to concentrate on. Very many of our troubles come to us through people. They hurt us, persecute us, and try our patience to the limit. Use this time, then, to learn lessons on how to live at peace with people (verse 14a). God sent you his trial through people so that you might better learn how to get alongside others and to be more winsome, reasonable, compassionate, caring, unselfish, and considerate. All those qualities will make you a better servant of his, a better ambassador, a better soul winner, a better example. Use the trouble which comes to you through people to develop those very qualities.

'The other thing to concentrate on is holiness of character (14b). In our lives there are thoughts, motives, attitudes, habits, priorities, loves, hates, trusts, opinions, and many other things that grieve the Lord. He sends us our painful experiences so that we can see how false many of our thoughts, words, and actions really are. Our minds are not in tune with his, and in difficulty we see this more clearly than ever. From all this, learn to be more holy.

'And know this: progress in holiness is not an optional extra but an absolute necessity, for without it no one—no one at all—will see the Lord. Are you someone who is not going forward in holiness? Then you are out of the race, unless you repent. Without holiness you will never reach the tape and enjoy the reward.'

(iii.) *And all the time watch out for dangers by the way* (verses 15-17)

12:15: 'Remember, you are not just running this race on your own. Do not keep an eye only on yourself, then, but conscientiously keep an eye on the rest of the pack. Is there anyone running with you who is showing signs of leaving the track, of falling short of the grace of God?

'Not only so, along the side of this course are thorn bushes of various sorts. Keep clear of them, for if you were to be pricked by the thorn of bitterness you would catch an infection that would quickly spread to others; and then how would you manage to finish the race?'

12:16-17: 'Forget the picture language and let me be straight with you: once you love *anything* more than you love God's blessing, it will be all up with you, whether it be sexual immorality, or living without the Lord, or whatever it may be. Do everything you can to make sure that there is nobody like that among you!

'Think of Esau and be warned! He was due for a blessing, but there was something which mattered to him much more. There was something *here and now* which was very much more important to him than all that God had in line for him in the future (*Gen.* 25:29-34).

'Esau turned his back on the blessing just so that everything could be as he wanted it here and now. Later on, however, he began to realise just what he had done. But it was too late. He had crossed the invisible line of no return. No amount of remorse, regret, crying, pleading, desire, or tears could ever restore to him what he had despised and lost. Nothing could bring it back.

'He chose to think little of the things of God and found himself condemned to walk along the path he had chosen—that of living and dying without the Lord. That, dear friends, is the peril of apostasy!'

21

HIGHER PRIVILEGES AND GREATER RESPONSIBILITIES

Please Read Hebrews 12:18-29

In our study of the Epistle to the Hebrews we now come to what is, in many ways, the climax of the epistle.

These Hebrews, you will remember, were Jews who had become Christians, but who were now thinking of giving it all up and returning to Judaism. This was mostly because the persecutions and difficulties that Christians have to face were too much for them. The apostle has therefore reminded them of why there have to be difficulties in the Christian life, and has warned them again that if they fail to make spiritual progress until the very end, they will certainly be lost.

What will the apostle say to them next? In today's passage he will concentrate on teaching two important lessons. In verses 18-24 he will explain that it is better to be a Christian than a Jew; and then in verses 25-29 he will stress that the higher are your privileges, the greater will be your responsibility.

1. It is better to be a Christian than a Jew (12:18-24)

The apostle makes this point in a most ingenious way. He compares two mountains and shows how that it is much better to be on one than on the other. He does not name the first mountain, although it is perfectly clear that it is Mount Sinai. This is where the Lord gave to Israel the Ten Commandments, as well as a great deal of additional legislation for the ancient nation. The apostle uses Mount Sinai as a symbol to show what Judaism is really like and what it has to offer.

The second mountain is Mount Zion—the crag on which Jerusalem is built. Going to Jerusalem and to the temple was a very different experience from being exposed to the terrors of Sinai. What a joy it was to go there with the happy pilgrims who came in crowds at the time of the annual feasts! And yet (as has often been explained in the epistle) all those Old Testament feasts and experiences were nothing more than pictures and symbols of heavenly realities.

Earthly Zion was utterly different from quaking Sinai. But it is not an earthly Zion that we believers have come to, but the true Zion and the heavenly Jerusalem. *That* is how much better the blessings of the gospel are over those provided by the law. *That* explains why it is better to be a Christian than a Jew.

Let us now work through the apostle's argument to see how he brings all of this out:

(i.) *Mount Sinai* (verses 18-21)

Mount Sinai was tangible (verse 18). It was a place of terrifying manifestations which could be detected by the bodily senses—namely, burning fire, a whirlwind, darkness, and a storm. What was experienced there more or less sums up the whole of the old dispensation. It was preoccupied with the material; with what can be seen, felt, heard, smelt, or tasted. By contrast, the gospel is wholly taken up with what is spiritual. People do not experience Sinai-like manifestations when they become new creatures in Christ.

Mount Sinai was a terrifying mountain (verses 19-21). God spoke audibly with an intelligible voice, and the terror-stricken people pleaded that in future he should only speak to them through a mediator. Even Moses was afraid and trembled—in giving us this information the apostle quotes from the *Septuagint*,[1] as well as referring to a Jewish tradition that was evidently true. It was not an inviting place. No one could approach God, except Moses and Aaron; and if so much as an animal went near, it was to be put to death!

It is not to Mount Sinai that we Christians have come, but to something completely different. The gospel we cherish is tender and welcoming: it invites us to 'come boldly' to the throne of grace (4:16) and to 'draw near' (10:22). In contrast to the exclusions of Sinai, it speaks of access. Instead of a terrifying voice, it assures us that God may be known as a heavenly Father. All this, and more, is brought out in the paragraph that follows.

(ii.) *Mount Zion* (verses 22-24)

When we came to Christ, we did not come to Sinai (to be terrified), but to Zion (to be welcomed). The Jewish mind associated Zion with welcome, because of the way pilgrims were welcomed to the annual feasts there, and because of the heart-warming memories that these pilgrimages repeatedly gave.

Unlike what happened at Sinai, we have not come to stand on the fringe. We have come to God's own dwelling place. The Jews reckoned that Jerusalem was where God's presence was to be found; but the apostle is not talking about an earthly city, but of the heavenly Jerusalem symbolised by that earthly city (verse 22). We must never forget that Old Testament Jerusalem had no importance, except as a picture of a heavenly reality. This explains why the New Testament consistently insists that prophecies supposedly having a Jewish fulfilment are actually fulfilled in the fortunes of the church,[2] where God dwells in the hearts and gatherings of his believing people.

Jews could undoubtedly remember how they joyously went up to Jerusalem in crowds. What a procession of people it was! But the procession of believers on their spiritual pilgrimage is much better than that. It is accompanied by and surrounded with 'an innumerable company of angels'. It is made up of the vast living family of those whose names are written in heaven and who have Jesus as their family head and brother ('the firstborn'). The front of the procession is already in the heavenly Jerusalem, and so Christians can be said to be joined to 'the spirits of just men made perfect' (verses 22-23).

Yes, God is to be feared, as Sinai demonstrated; after all, he is 'the judge of all' (verse 23). But our privilege as believers is not to have shrunk from him, but to have come to him. This is because we have come to Jesus, whose human name we are not ashamed to use. And who is he? He is 'the mediator of the new covenant' (verse 24). By him we have entered into what we could never enter into if, like the Jews, we still relied on a covenant of works. We have come to his blood. It has been sprinkled on us for our cleansing. It is not a blood that cries out for vengeance and punishment, as Abel's did. We are talking about the life-blood which he shed for us on his cross, and which speaks therefore of pardon, forgiveness, acceptance, peace with God, and access—in short, it speaks of *welcome*.

It would be fair to summarise the apostle's reasoning something like this:

> 12:18-24: 'Judaism could bring you, and *did* bring you, no further than those people who stood distant and afraid at the foot of Sinai. But look where the gospel has brought you! All those Old Testament feasts and pilgrimages were but pictures of this glorious reality. So why turn your back on that which is obviously better, to return to something clearly imperfect?'

What a spirit of triumph and joy there is in this paragraph! Who can fully recite the blessings of the Christian life? Why would any one ever consider turning their back on them? Where else can such blessings and joys be found? No wonder that chapter 12 has been described by so many as the climax of the epistle!

2. The higher your privileges, the greater your responsibility (12:25-29)

12:25: 'Oh Christians, Christians, the God who has done all this for you is speaking to you! You seem to have made up your mind to turn your back on all these blessings, and to have closed your ears to all appeals to do otherwise. But don't close your ears to him. He is speaking to you!

'When he spoke on earth (that is, from Sinai), those who refused to hear what he had to say did not get away with it. If that was true then, how much more is it true now that he speaks from heaven!'

Sinai was a great act of condescension on God's part. He no longer speaks in that way; rather, he speaks from heaven, to where his Son has ascended. He speaks as his Word is announced by his servants and as his Spirit applies it to the minds and consciences of the hearers.

We must note that the glory of this gospel dispensation is not less, but greater, as we have constantly learned in our study of this epistle. It was serious to refuse the Lord in Old Testament times, but it is infinitely more serious to refuse him now. What attention we should give to his Word as it is read in public, and when we read it for ourselves! And what attention we should give as Christ-sent men preach it!

12:26: 'Once his voice shook the earth, as happened at Sinai. But do you remember what God said through his prophet Haggai? His promise was, "Yet once more I shake (or, will shake) not only the earth, but also heaven."'[3]

12:27: 'Think about those words, "Yet once more . . ." Those things which can be shaken are one day going to be shaken away. They will be removed. I am talking about the physical creation; the visible earth and heavens will one day pass away, and this will be brought about by the action of God. When that occurs, as it will, only those things which cannot be shaken will remain. I am, of course, talking about those spiritual realities of which everything in the Old Testament was only a picture.'

The time is coming when all the earthly pictures, and the earth itself, as well as the whole physical universe as we know it, will be no more. All that will then remain will be spiritual realities, namely God, the angels, and men and women. That day will be the downfall of every materialist; they will have nothing left. It will also be the downfall of every Jew who has spent his life engrossed with sacrifice, ritual, ceremony, the priesthood, and the whole paraphernalia of outward religious glory, rather than the eternal spiritual realities which are symbolised by these things. Everything he lived for will be gone—all gone, and gone for ever!

12:28: 'If you are not a member of God's spiritual kingdom, where, oh where, will you then be? You will be naked before God with nowhere to flee. But, thanks be to God, the gospel has made us members of a spiritual kingdom. We are his accepted people, over whom he rules. This kingdom, being spiritual in nature, will not be shaken by coming events, and will remain. When all else has gone, we will be safe.

'This being so, "let us have grace", by which I mean, let us show gratitude and render thanks (in the same way as "saying grace" at meals is expressing gratitude). In this way we will serve God acceptably, with reverence and godly fear.'

The apostle is reminding us of the truth about the universe. Everything that we know, except for spiritual beings and realities, is going to pass away. This being so, we should make it our chief business to have dealings with God, thanking him for his mercy, spending all our days serving him, and reverencing him; that is, living lives characterised by affectionate fear for him.

> 12:29: 'The alternative—that of living and dying in a way that is not pleasing to him—is too awful to contemplate. It would mean witnessing the disappearance of heaven and earth, and seeing all my hopes disappearing with them. With nowhere to hide, I would then find myself alone with a consuming fire!'

These things being so, how can any of us think of deserting the Christian life, of going back to what we were before, of pleasing ourselves, of turning our backs on Christ, and of being the same as everybody else—living entirely for what we can see, or hear, or smell, or taste, or handle?

How can we think of anything else, except *pleasing him?*

22

HOW TO LIVE AS A CHRISTIAN

Please Read Hebrews 13:1-6

For twelve chapters the apostle has been parading before us the glories of the Lord Jesus Christ and the blessings that have come to us through him. He has pleaded with us not to turn our backs on him and has bluntly warned us that, if we do, there is only one place that awaits us: outer darkness. He has shown to us that until our dying moment we must go on and on, making definite and forward steps in spiritual progress.

It is in this spirit that he now writes his closing chapter. It consists of a number of brief statements that point out particular areas which require special attention, if indeed we are to make spiritual progress. So where does he begin?

1. Give special attention to your relationships with other Christians (13:1-3)

13:1: 'The attitude that must prevail here is one of brotherly love. I am not telling you to *consider* yourselves to be brothers and to behave accordingly. No, no! I am instructing you to remember the *fact* that you are brothers and to give yourself to a practical display of that fact.'

The Christian church is not an organisation, a society, or a club. It is a brotherhood. All believers—even the ones that we do not like!—are our brothers. This is a fact. It is not a matter in which we have any choice. We are not to behave as *if* this were true, but to remember that this *is* true—there are a million miles between these two mindsets. Every Christian, man or woman, is a brother, whether I treat him or her rightly or not. Every failure in my relationships with fellow-Christians is a sin against a brother, and is therefore a grief to our heavenly Father.

> 13:2: 'This brotherliness extends not only to the members of your home church who, of course, you know well. It embraces all believers, even those who are strangers to you and who are just passing through. Be hospitable to them.'

We can see what the apostle is saying, but what does it actually mean in practice? It is easy to answer this. I simply have to ask myself how I would treat my physical brother if he turned up unannounced at church. *That* is how I am to treat my spiritual brothers.

Hospitality was particularly important in the world of the first century. Most inns and lodging places were basic and uncomfortable, and many of them were places of low repute. The New Testament therefore underlines the importance of the Christian home and portrays it as a place that is to be open to everyone in the Lord's family. Who can tell how many lives have thus been strengthened, enriched, and transformed through the centuries, right up to today?

> 'And remember, it is not just the guests who benefit. By being hospitable, some believers have had the extraordinary privilege of unwittingly entertaining angels!'

The apostle's point is that hospitable people are often rewarded with marvellous surprises. Both Abraham and Lot received actual angels into their homes, unaware, at least to begin with, that they were entertaining angels.[1] I do not believe that the apostle is teaching us to expect a similar blessing, although it is not impossible.

But who knows who the next guest will be, or what blessings might come as a result?

> 13:3: 'But how about the Christians that you never meet? They are just as much your brothers too. Do not forget this, especially when it concerns those who are in prison or who are being ill-treated for their faith. It could just as easily be *you* who had to go through this experience.'

If I heard today that my physical brother was in prison, what would I do? I would immediately place myself in his shoes (verse 3a). I would think of what he might need, whether it be help, letters, a visit, clothes, paper, books, or whatever. I would then think of his loved ones—his wife, children, and wider family—and would set out to ring them, visit them, supply their needs or take them on holiday. My mind would be filled with loving and practical thoughts.

It is to be no different with my spiritual brothers. They are not in prison as criminals, but because they have been faithful to the Lord Jesus Christ. It could just as easily be me! It is no good saying to myself, 'I don't know them.' They are my brothers! What am I doing?

And what would I do today if I heard that my physical brother was being ill-treated? I would immediately think of what it must be like, remembering that if I have not been through the same experience, I am certainly not exempt from it (verse 3b). I would ring him, visit him, spiritually encourage him, keep him up with the news if he is out of action, and do everything I could to care for his family too. I would not say, 'I have another brother, let him look after this one.' No, I would take steps to do something myself, however much my other brother was doing.

The work of ministering to the imprisoned and suffering is not the work of one particular brother, but of the whole family. And yet lots and lots of believers are today languishing for lack of proper pastoral care because the myth has got round (in total contradiction to the Word of God) that they are more the concern of some members of the fellowship (such as the pastor and elders) than of others.

The day I treat all other believers for what they are—brothers!—not only will my own spiritual life make progress, but so will theirs. Yes, we are to recognise that spiritual ties are stronger than any ties found in a natural family, and we are to act accordingly. Our relationships with other Christians are of vital importance. 'Let brotherly love continue.'

2. Give special attention not to be infected by worldly attitudes (13:4-6)

The apostle now draws attention to two common attitudes which will destroy any Christian's testimony before the world, unless he gets rid of them. One is a certain attitude to marriage (verse 4). The other is a certain attitude to money (verses 5-6).

It seems almost incredible that the apostle wrote these verses nearly two thousand years ago! His comments are as relevant to us today as they ever were to the original readers.

(i.) Our attitude to marriage (13:4)

In the depraved world of the first century the marriage bond meant very little. Who cared about marriage? As a result, sexual intercourse between unmarried people was rife, as were adultery and homosexuality. This situation caused some Christians to over-react. They taught that sexual purity was of such importance that the gospel demanded celibacy and asceticism—Christians should not marry, should not have anything to do with sex, and should treat their bodies harshly.

Faced with these two extremes, it is wonderful to see how balanced the apostle's teaching is. He asserts that there is nothing dishonourable about the marriage relationship. How could there be, seeing that God ordained it? Physical intimacy within marriage is his gift. There is nothing defiling about it and it is to be enjoyed. The Lord's way is chastity *outside* the marriage bond and enjoyment *within* it—and what a wonderful witness this has been through the centuries. Consistent Christians are faithful and loving partners who create and maintain stable and loving homes.

All who engage in improper sexual relationships, whether they be unmarried or married, have God against them—as they will discover at the last judgement. Sexually immoral and liberal people will one day have to answer for their thoughts, words, and deeds, and will do so before an angry God! Think of it! Society's voices are loud and persuasive, but it is not at last to society that we are accountable, but to the God who created us and instructed how we should live. In Jesus Christ there is pardon for all who have failed, as this Epistle to the Hebrews has repeatedly made clear. But in times of strong temptation we must all learn to say with Joseph, 'How then can I do this great wickedness, and sin against God?' (*Gen.* 39:9).

(ii.) *Our attitude to money* (13:5-6)

However, the God who said, 'You shall not commit adultery' also said, 'You shall not covet . . .' (*Exod.* 20:14, 17), thus showing that jealous eagerness for material possessions is as wicked as sexual sin. There is widespread resistance to this fact, but it remains a fact nonetheless. The apostle's words here refer to covetousness in general, and to loving money in particular. Christian conduct is to be just as free from material discontentment as it is from sexual immorality.

God's way for us is contentment, not covetousness. It means 'making do' and not 'wanting more'. This attitude is possible because, as God's children, we do not face life alone. The Lord has promised to each one of us his personal help. He will never leave any of us in the lurch. Unconverted people take comfort from their possessions. They find their security in remembering how much they own. We are not like that. We take comfort from the fact that God is with us, providing for us, and that he will never leave us or forsake us.

What a challenge this is to a materialistic age like our own, where very little seems to matter to people except how much they earn and how much they have got. When their financial security is threatened, people all around us find that they cannot cope. Meanwhile we can face life cheerfully. We can boldly and confidently say that the Lord is at our side, that there is therefore nothing to fear and nobody who can finally harm us. Having him, we shall always have enough. It was not in vain that our Lord said to us, 'Do not worry . . . for your heavenly Father knows that you need all these things. But seek first the kingdom of God and his righteousness, and all these things shall be added to you. Therefore do not worry about tomorrow, for tomorrow will worry about its own things. Sufficient for the day is its own trouble' (*Matt.* 6:25, 32-34).

We each need to ask ourselves how much progress we are making in the two areas that the apostle has identified, and to keep giving special attention not to be infected by the world's attitudes to marriage and to money.

We each need an antiseptic which, if regularly applied, would prevent the world's infection from spreading in us, and which would eventually drive it away. The formula for this antiseptic consists in exposing our mind less to the world's mind (especially as transmitted by the media, with their 'soaps',[2] comedy programmes, and quiz shows offering fabulous prizes); by fleeing people and places which stir up sexual and financial lust; and by exposing our mind very much more to God's mind (especially as transmitted by the preached Word, but also by the reading of Scripture and good Christian books, and spiritually strengthening friendships), accompanying everything with prayer. In addition, most Christians should marry, and should then cultivate their marriages so as to enjoy them increasingly. Finally, all of us should give more of our money away to the Lord's work and to the Lord's needy people.

If all believers lived in line with the first six verses of this chapter, their lives would be revolutionised and the watching world would be astonished. Caring, loving people, with pure minds, settled marriages, and happy families cannot fail to impress. The effect is even greater when it is realised that they are like that because they think more of the next life than the present one, and their single desire at all times is to please the God who has redeemed them. But there is more than this to be said about living the Christian life, as our further study of this final chapter will reveal.

23

AUTHORITY AND SPIRITUALITY

PLEASE READ HEBREWS 13:7-8, 17

In his final chapter the apostle is talking about Christian behaviour and is pointing out a number of areas to which we should give special attention if we are to make spiritual progress. He has already mentioned our relationships with other Christians and the danger of being infected with worldly attitudes, but two other areas are also in his mind. The first of these concerns having a proper attitude to our leaders, both past and present, while never losing sight of the ultimate leader.

3. Give special attention to having a proper attitude to Christian leaders (13:7-8, 17)

(i.) *Past leaders* (verse 7)

On first sight this verse appears to be about people who are still living. It accurately translates the Greek by saying to us, 'Remember those who rule over you.' This phrase, however, undoubtedly means, 'Remember your leaders', as the NIV puts it. As we read the whole verse, it becomes clear that it is past leaders who are being referred to. They are those who 'have spoken the word of God' and whose 'exit' (Greek) has been recorded. In using this term the apostle is speaking of the end of their earthly life. We can therefore paraphrase the whole verse like this:

13:7: 'In the past you have had wonderful leaders. Call them to mind. They were men of faith, noted for presenting a true message and giving a godly example. Consider afresh the lives that they lived and the way that their lives ended and, instead of giving up the faith and life in which they instructed you, copy that faith and follow that example. In short, imitate them.'

What the apostle is commanding is a tremendous antidote to apostasy. Oh, the godly men and women we have been privileged to know! What lives they lived! We have never seen their like anywhere else. And what deaths they died! They left the world filled with faith and hope. We have never seen deaths like theirs.

These godly examples are to us a demonstration of the power of the gospel. They confirm and strengthen our faith in it. Apostasy, Judaism, or any other belief system, is simply unable to produce men and women like that. Their fragrant lives have left on us an indelible impression that makes us want to be like them, and steals from us all desire to be like other people. How poor are other lives compared with theirs!

If we combine the memories of any group of Christians, we will find that we can call to mind the names and examples of hundreds of believers who are now safely with the Lord. As we remember how they ran the race and have entered into their reward, we find that we ourselves are spurred on to run well and to finish the race. We should not be ashamed of our walks down memory lane. We are commanded to remember such people, especially those who were our leaders and from whose lips we heard the Word of God, and to follow their example.

(ii.) *Present leaders* (verse 17)

Such leaders have gone, never to return, and we miss them still. But, for all that, the church of Christ is not leaderless. This is because the Lord is faithful to his promises, such as 'Instead of your fathers shall be your sons, whom you shall make princes in all the earth' (*Psa.* 45:16) and 'One generation shall praise your works to another, and shall declare your mighty acts' (*Psa.* 145:4).

Moses is followed by Joshua, Elijah by Elisha, and Paul by Timothy. In mourning those who have gone from us, we must in no way look down on those leaders whom God has appointed to replace them. Our deceased leaders were called for their time, and our present leaders are called 'for such a time as this' (*Esther* 4:14). We must not forget that God was with Joshua as he was with Moses (*Josh.* 1:5) and that those who mock new leaders are judged by God, as the fate of the youths who insulted Elisha clearly proves (*2 Kings* 2:23-25). Just as it is our duty to reflect on our former leaders, it is our duty to have a right attitude to our present ones.

That duty is to 'obey' them and to 'be submissive' to them (verse 17). The apostle is not telling us to treat them as sergeants or school teachers. It is possible to comply with the instructions of such people, and at the same time to curse them inwardly, because of our unbroken will and unloving heart. The obedience required here is a voluntary one. Recognising that Christ has structured his church in a certain way, we willingly put ourselves under the authority of those whom he has appointed to rule and to teach. Their authority is a delegated authority and is not absolute, and it extends only to areas of biblical understanding and godly behaviour. This we recognise. But it is a real authority and, out of love for Christ, we submit to it most gladly.

It needs to be said that some readers of this book cannot possibly obey this command because, despite their Christian profession, they flit from church to church and are not church members anywhere. They have never been to a group of godly local church leaders and asked them to shepherd their souls. This is a failure to which they must give attention and for which they must repent.

But why are spiritual leaders to be obeyed and submitted to so freely? It is because we are all prone to wander from the Lord, as this epistle has constantly underlined. We need someone to watch over us. All of us are to do this for each other (3:13; 10:25), but Christ has appointed the elders of local congregations to be especially responsible for this task. At the last judgement they will have to give an account of how well they have done it. They will be answerable to the Lord for the example they have shown, the teaching of the church that they have organised and given, and the pastoral care they have practised. What an enormous responsibility is theirs!

How much easier their task is when every individual in the church gives them the respect that they deserve, imitates their good example, and submits willingly to their lead. The work of elders is difficult enough; why should we make it *more* difficult? Why not rather make their work a joy? We can do this by recognising them as leaders, by submitting to their teaching at every point where it is biblical, and by being open with them about everything that bears upon the welfare of our own soul, or upon the welfare of others in the church.

It is not hard to bring grief into the heart of a true pastor, but this verse forbids us to do it. We grieve our leaders when we do not respect them, when we live as if we were not accountable to anyone, when we never inform them beforehand of our absences, and when we obviously resent as obtrusive their concerned questions. The fact remains, however, that they remain responsible for our pastoral care, whether we grieve them or not. So let us submit to them, and thus help them to do their job with joy. The more we co-operate with them, the better their care will be. Any other attitude is 'not profitable for you', says the apostle.

(iii.) *The ultimate leader* (verse 8)

In looking at human leaders, past and present, it is vital that we should not take our eyes off the ultimate leader. How appropriate it is that verse 8 should be included in this section! It is consistent with the spirit of the whole epistle, which has constantly paraded Christ's glories before us and has told us never to take our eyes off him, reminding us that this is the only way to keep going spiritually, and not to be lost. Nonetheless, when we first read chapter 12, we have the impression that verse 8 does not quite 'fit'. Why exactly is it there?

A few moments reflection will give us the answer. The apostle has been talking about past leaders and present leaders. As he has done so, your mind might have been asking, 'But what about the future? Can we be sure that there will be suitable leaders then?'

Where did our past leaders come from? The ascended Christ raised them up and gave them to his church, as is explained in detail in Ephesians 4:7-16. Where do our present leaders come from? They come from the same source. The good news is that 'Jesus Christ is the same yesterday, today, and for ever.' Our Lord remains unchanged. This is the guarantee that leaders will not be lacking in the future.

There is too much fear in the church. Our thoughts run away with us. We miss the fine leaders who have gone to glory and we know that some of our best present leaders will soon be gone too. Many others to whom we looked with respect and affection have let us down by their moral offences and indiscretions. Who will let us down next? How will our churches cope when such-and-such retires, dies, or moves on? All these fears spring from our forgetting who the real Head of the church is. He is the one who never changes, never lets us down, never goes away, and whose power is always available. In a world where everything is changing, what strength and relief we find in reciting verse 8!

The moment we forget this brief verse, our attitude to our leaders is certain to be wrong. We are prone to idolise them; this verse reminds us that they are but mortal under-shepherds and that he is the permanent Head. We are prone to criticise them; but once we remember that they are the servants that he has sent, we are moved to put a curb on our tongues. At the last day it is to him, not to them, that we shall answer.

We follow our leaders, but only as much as they follow Christ (*1 Cor.* 4:16; 11:1). Human leaders come and go, but the great Exemplar remains. The great saints and leaders in the Bible and in church history had no spiritual life, no sustaining grace, and no power to persevere, except what they received from Christ. Christ is unchanged, so what they received from him we may receive too. He may not give us the same gifts, but there is no reason why we cannot live with equal holiness. All the resources they enjoyed are available to us as well. Whatever the Lord Jesus Christ has been to one sinner, he is able and willing to be to any sinner.

That is how it was yesterday, that is how it is today, and that is how it will be tomorrow. If, spiritually, we are not what we should be, it is not because Christ has changed. The fault lies squarely with us. We have chosen the path of refusing intimate communion with the Lord, although our opportunity to be holy and persevering is as large as that of any person in history.

24

CONCLUDING EXHORTATIONS
AND BENEDICTIONS

Please Read Hebrews 13:9-16, 18-25

As we have seen, the last chapter of Hebrews consists of a number of brief statements pointing us to particular areas of our Christian life and experience which require special attention. Of the four areas identified, we have examined three. We are to give special attention to our relationships with other Christians (verses 1-3), to not being infected with worldly attitudes (verses 4-6) and to having a proper attitude to our spiritual leaders (verses 7-8, 17).

We have now studied the whole of the epistle except for 13:9-16 and 13:18-25. The first of these sections points us to the fourth area which requires our special attention, while the remaining section consists of concluding exhortations, including some greetings, and of benedictions.

4. Give special attention to grasping the fact that Christianity is essentially a spiritual religion (13:9-16)

13:9: This verse is a warning. Circulating among the readers were all sorts of strange teachings which perverted the truth and were likely to lead them away from the gospel. One of them was the idea that you can get nowhere in the Christian life unless you partake of special, sacred, sacrificial food. This idea no doubt had its roots in the Book of Leviticus where, after certain sacrifices, the worshipper ate the animal he had offered, or at least parts of it, and also shared the meat with others. By teaching that something similar is the way to spiritual progress, this idea perverted the gospel, compromised with Judaism, and gave tacit approval to a continuation of the old sacrificial system.

What is the apostle's reaction to this error? He tells his readers not to be carried away by weird notions. You are strengthened in the Christian life, not by what you eat or do not eat, but by God's working in your heart. This is proved by the fact that those who embrace this error and who eat the specified food do not, in fact, profit as a result.

In saying this, the apostle shows the way forward for us all. Our great need is not to adopt certain outward practices, but to be strengthened inwardly and spiritually. Christianity has no interest in externals. The idea that going through certain rituals, or practising dietary rules, does us good and is somehow pleasing to God, is an idea completely foreign to the religion of the New Testament. It is the heart that matters. What is going on deep down inside us? How are we getting on in personal faith, in love for Christ, in understanding his Word, in resisting temptation, in inward holiness, and in love for others?—these are the questions that matter, and have to be answered.

13:10-14: Not all Old Testament sacrifices, however, required the worshipper to eat something. The sin offering is an obvious example (*Lev.* 4). There the animal was killed on the altar, but no one ate any part of it, not even the priests who served in the tabernacle. The blood of the sacrificed animals was brought into the sanctuary to make atonement for sin, but the bodies were not eaten. The fat and some inward parts were burned on the altar, while the bodies were burned outside the camp (verse 11).

Everything about that sin offering spoke of our Lord Jesus Christ. Our interest is not in the altars of the Old Testament, but in the altar which people who practise only the outward forms of Levitical religion have no right to come to (verse 10). Our altar is Christ. That is why it would be categorically wrong for any of us to erect any other sort of altar today. His blood was shed once for all (as Hebrews has frequently explained) to set apart his people for God. It was not in earthly Jerusalem that he suffered, but outside it, thus setting aside all the Levitical rituals going on in that city. Redemption was accomplished without any reference whatever to them (verse 12).

All this means two things for believers (verse 13). First of all, it means that we reject Judaism; let us join our Saviour outside the camp and have nothing further to do with Levitical rites and ceremonies. Secondly, it means that the Jews reject us. They despised our Lord and cast him out, just as they cast out the dead bodies of their sacrifices. Let us carry that reproach and openly identify ourselves with our Lord 'outside the camp'.

This reproach is not such a hard thing to bear (verse 14). Any reproach we bear in this life will soon be over. We are not on this earth for ever. We will soon be in heaven. Our hopes are not set on any earthly city and on what goes on there. Everything relating to this earthly order will soon be gone. Our hopes are all in a city which is soon to become visible, the heavenly Jerusalem (which we learned about in 12:22). That city will remain when everything else has passed away (12:27).

13:15-16: There is, then, no place for the Christian to have *anything* to do with the Levitical sacrificial system. The sacrifices which we offer are of a different order altogether. Through the mediation of Christ, and by that alone, we bring our offerings to God—and it is something that the apostle urges us to do continually. But our offerings are not blood-sacrifices. They are found on our lips and consist of praise to God and thanks to his name.

In addition, we bring our sacrifices of love. These consist of our good deeds and especially of the way we spend our lives meeting the needs of others. Such sacrifices bring real pleasure to the heart of God.

This remarkable paragraph is a key passage for all who would truly understand Christianity. It has no interest whatever in rites and ceremonies. It is what is going on in the heart that matters.

Does Christianity have any sort of altar or sacrificial system? No! The only altar on which an acceptable sacrifice has ever been offered is that of Calvary. The only sin offering which has ever accomplished anything is Christ's once for all, never to be repeated sacrifice there. He is also the high priest who carried out the sacrifice and who now successfully intercedes for sinners as he sits permanently in the only true Holy of Holies, the very presence of God.

This means that Christians erect no altars, kill no sacrifices, and ordain no priests. All these things are superfluous and have passed away. Our hopes do not depend on any of those things, but on the Lord Jesus Christ. All that matters is a personal relationship with him. We therefore have nothing further to do with what he has rendered redundant. We are glad to openly identify ourselves with him, although this brings upon us all sorts of reproach.

Does this mean, then, that Christians do not offer any sacrifices? No! But our sacrifices are bloodless, consisting of worshipful and thankful fellowship with God, and of the unselfish and sacrificial life-style which the indwelling Spirit of Christ produces within us.

Christianity, then, is not a religion of forms and ceremonies, offerings and liturgies, priests and mysteries, do's and don'ts, altars and candles, robes, plates, incense, crosses, pictures, icons, bells, sacrifices, or anything remotely similar. Any religion which gives attention to these things is not Christianity, which is concerned with God's gift of grace in the heart. Its characteristics are trust in the finished work of Christ and open allegiance to him, together with the bearing of the reproach that this brings. It longs for heaven, communes with the God of heaven, approaches him constantly through Christ, is filled with overflowing praise and thankfulness to him, and, for his sake, lives for the welfare of others.

If you, dear reader, have not grasped this, it is because you are not a Christian at all. There is no hope of your making spiritual progress, because you have not yet begun the race. Having read this far, it is certainly time for you to turn away from all externals and to embrace the Lord Jesus Christ in your heart. Christianity is essentially a *spiritual* religion.

Concluding exhortations, including greetings, and benedictions (13:18-25)

(i.) *Exhortations* (verses 18-19, 22-24)

13:18: Here for the last time in the epistle, the writer speaks of himself. He cannot close his letter of teaching, warning, and encouragement without confessing his need of prayer. He has sometimes been very blunt with his readers and knows that his attitude and action may have been misunderstood. He therefore assures us that he is doing his best to keep a clear conscience and to be above board in everything.

13:19: But he has one particular prayer request, and it is that he may be with his readers sooner rather than later. Where, precisely, is the apostle as he writes? Is he in prison? In the light of verse 23, this seems unlikely. Is he ill? Not as far as we know. Why then does he pray to be 'restored' to his readers? It is not a question that we can answer with any certainty. All we know is that he had been separated from them, and that he is now asking for them to pray that he may be restored to them the sooner.

Verses 18-19 have something to teach us. This great teacher of the Christian faith is a humble man: he feels his need of prayer. He is a sensitive man: sensitive to how his readers may be receiving his letter. He is also a prayerful man: who else would ask for prayer and, especially, for very specific requests to be made on his behalf?

13:22: In verse 22 he claims to have written 'in few words'. For ourselves, we may be inclined to disagree with him, seeing it has taken us some time to read his letter of thirteen chapters and to study it! However, considering the vastness of its themes, it *is* a brief letter, and he asks them to 'bear with' his word of exhortation, that is, to give it their full attention.

Is this something that we, in turn, are willing to do? As we near the end of the epistle, how seriously are we taking its message, its warnings and its encouragements? What definite steps are we taking to remember its main truths and to put into practice its obvious lessons? Which of these steps are we going to take first?

13:23: This said, the apostle immediately gives a further exhortation, although it is slightly veiled. He instructs his readers to be 'in the know' as far as news of other Christians is concerned. On this occasion he wants them to take note of the fact that Timothy has been set free, presumably from prison, and that he intends to come with him to visit them. There have been a few personal touches here and there in Hebrews, and here is one more. Personal comments like these cause the epistle to have a more human tone, and make us inclined to receive it as the personal letter it is, rather than as some sort of impersonal circular.

13:24: There is no substitute for personal touches, but when they are not possible, we must do the best that we can. So the apostle sends very general greetings to the leaders and to all Hebrew Christians. In addition, he passes on the greetings of believers in Italy, from where, perhaps, he is writing.

However, exhortations and greetings without some expressed desire for the Lord's blessing make a letter a very cold affair. No mature Christian would want to close a letter like that. So it is that we conclude by considering the two benedictions which are found in this closing paragraph.

(ii.) *Benedictions* (25, 20-21)

13:25: The Epistle closes with the simple benediction of verse 25. In the light of 13:9 its wording is perfectly understandable. More than anything else, what the apostle wants for all his readers is that they should experience that undeserved, inward, spiritually transforming, personally strengthening work of God that the New Testament often calls 'grace'. Surely that is what every believer wants for himself and for others! The closing benediction can be so brief because, just before it, he has given something much more comprehensive—one of the most wonderful benedictions in the whole of Scripture.

13:20-21: It is a benediction that focuses the Hebrews' thoughts on the doings of God. To those who are tempted to go back to a religion of no access, simply because they want to avoid the persecution and discouragement of the Christian life, he reminds them that their God is 'the God of peace'. This God has brought up again from the dead the Lord Jesus, not just as a private individual, but as the leader or shepherd of his people, his sheep. What the apostle is conveying is that they, as those who belong to Christ, may expect the same thing to happen to them. Because they are Christians they can, and should, look beyond death and beyond the resurrection.

Christ's resurrection followed his death. The spilling of his blood did not take place in accordance with Jewish rites, but because of what was decided in 'the everlasting covenant'. Jewish rites and sacrifices were shadows based on that covenant, and not vice-versa. Christianity is not a departure from a divine institution, but the true expression of the covenant that God made within himself before the world was made. The benefits secured by Christ cannot therefore fail. His blood was 'the blood of the everlasting covenant' and, unlike the blood of Old Testament sacrifices, will never give place to something else or to something better.

This said, the apostle prays that the God of peace and power and love will make his readers complete, and free from anything defective, lacking, or weak; and that this will extend to every aspect of their lives. He prays for this in order that they may spend their lives doing God's will, and therefore pleasing him. He will bring this about by working in them. Their lives will thus be the outflow of the divine change inside. As they live consciously in God's sight, they will please him very much.

In short, the apostle is praying that his readers may make definite progress in the things of God, both in their understanding and in action. He prays through Jesus Christ, knowing that it is from him that all blessings flow. He has spent his whole letter fixing their attention on him, and does it one final time by adding, 'to whom be glory for ever and ever.'

The apostatising heart is not interested in giving everlasting glory to the Lord Jesus Christ. The backsliding heart knows that it should do so, but does not do anything about it. But when the heart of a progressing, persevering believer hears these final words, it bursts into an enthusiastic 'AMEN!'

ENDNOTES

PREFACE

[1] W. H. Griffith Thomas, *Hebrews : A Devotional Commentary* (Grand Rapids: Eerdmans, seventh printing, 1977).

[2] Thomas Hewitt, *The Epistle to the Hebrews: An Introduction and Commentary* (London: Tyndale Press, 1960).

[3] Irving L. Jensen, *Hebrews: A Self-Study Guide* (Chicago: Moody Press, 1970).

2

GOD HAS SPOKEN

[1] The outline I am presenting is that of W. H. Griffith Thomas (see Preface). The comment is mine.

[2] This is verse 2 of the hymn 'Once in royal David's city' by Cecil Frances Alexander (1818-95). It is No. 210 in *Christian Hymns* (Bridgend: Evangelical Movement of Wales, 2004).

[3] This chorus by Audrey Mieir (born 1916) is No. 922 in *Christian Hymns*.

3

TEACHING AND WARNING

[1] This well-known and biblically justified expression is from James Montgomery's hymn 'Hail to the Lord's Anointed', which is No. 467 in *Christian Hymns*.

5

THE PERIL OF APOSTASY

[1] This is from the hymn 'Mighty Christ from time eternal' by Titus Lewis (1773-1811) as translated by Graham Harrison. It is No. 168 in *Christian Hymns*.

[2] John Murray, *Redemption Accomplished and Applied,* (Edinburgh: Banner of Truth, 2009 reprint), p. 53.

6

THE PROMISED REST

[1] This is the chorus to Helen Howarth Lemmel's well-known hymn, 'O soul, are you wearied and troubled?' It is No. 265 in *The Christian Life Hymnal* (London: National Young Life Campaign, 1953).

[2] This is the second verse of 'O walk with Jesus' by Edwin Paxton Hood (1820-85). It is No. 557 in *Christian Hymns*.

7

CHRIST'S HIGH PRIESTHOOD

[1] 'Eternal generation' is the theological term for the Bible's teaching that the second person of the Trinity is, from all eternity, God. He is God in exactly the same way as the Father is God. He is God in his own right. And yet all that he is, he owes to God the Father, from whom he is distinct. This truth is only part of the mystery of the Trinity. Because of God's revelation, we may state what the truth is; but because of our creatureliness and our sin, we cannot fully grasp it.

11

A HIGH PRIEST FOREVER ACCORDING TO THE ORDER OF MELCHIZEDEK

[1] I am indebted to Irving L. Jensen for this outline (see Preface).

12

THE MEDIATOR OF A BETTER COVENANT

[1] This is the fourth verse of the anonymous hymn, 'All for Jesus! All for Jesus!' found in numerous hymnbooks published during the twentieth century.

13

THE PRIEST OF A BETTER TABERNACLE

[1] Once more I am indebted to W. H. Griffith Thomas for the outline that follows (see Preface).

[2] It is thanks to Irving L. Jensen that I first saw these points (see Preface).

14

THE OFFERER OF A BETTER SACRIFICE

[1] This is the second verse of the well-known hymn 'When I survey the wondrous cross' by Isaac Watts (1674-1748). It is No. 263 in *Christian Hymns*.

15

UNDERLINING AND ENFORCING

[1] The outline of this chapter is loosely but obviously based on W. H. Griffith Thomas (see Preface).

[2] This is the answer to Question 534 ('Is the Mass a mere remembrance of Calvary?') of *The St. Peter Catechism of Catholic Doctrine* approved by the Roman Catholic Church in the United Kingdom in 1972 (Liverpool and London: Print Origination, 1972, p. 49).

[3] This is C. I. Scofield's comment on Ezekiel 43:19 in *The Scofield Reference Bible* (New York: Oxford University Press, 1909, p. 890).

17

FAITH: DEFINED AND ILLUSTRATED

[1] NIV stands for the Holy Bible, New International Version, copyright © 1978, 1984 by International Bible Society, and is a registered trademark of the International Bible Society. It is published in the UK by Hodder and Stoughton.

[2] The NIV, which translates Hebrews 11:1 so well, is thoroughly misleading at this point. The commentary you are reading is based on the British usage edition of The Holy Bible, New King James Version (London, Samuel Bagster, 1982), © Thomas Nelson, Inc., 1982.

21

HIGHER PRIVILEGES AND GREATER RESPONSIBILITIES

[1] The *Septuagint* was the translation into Greek of the Hebrew Old Testament carried out in Alexandria, Egypt, in the third century B.C. The New Testament writers often quote from this version. Tradition says that the work was done by seventy Jewish scholars; hence the symbol LXX (Roman figures for 70) is often used when referring to the *Septuagint*.

[2] For example, compare Joel 2:28-32 with Acts 2:1-39, and Amos 9:11-12 with Acts 15:6-31.

[3] Haggai 2:6.

22

HOW TO LIVE AS A CHRISTIAN

[1] See Genesis chapters 18 and 19.

[2] A 'soap' or 'soap opera' is a long-running TV drama serial revolving round the lives of a group of people.